# A Mommy's Road

To Thea,

A Mommy's Road

Creative Approaches for Parenting

*Reflect
Renew
Rejuvenate*

Lori Koch

LORI KOCH

Edited by Lizzie Vance

Mill City Press
Minneapolis, MN

Copyright © 2015 by Lori Koch

MILL CITY PRESS

Mill City Press, Inc.
322 First Avenue N, 5th floor
Minneapolis, MN 55401
612.455.2293
www.millcitypublishing.com

All rights reserved. No part of this publication may be reproduced, stored in a retrieval system, or transmitted, in any form or by any means, electronic, mechanical, photocopying, recording, or otherwise, without the prior written permission of the author.

To contact Lori to book her for speaking engagements, call 888-964-4694
For more information, go to www.womenGIGS.com

ISBN-13: 978-1-63413-564-1
LCCN: 2015908151

Edited by Lizzie Vance
Book Design by Sophie Chi

Printed in the United States of America

Dedication

This book is dedicated to my supportive, loving husband, Dan. As I have persisted in my many crazy endeavors, he has always stood beside me. Dan, thank you for your commitment to me, your patience, and your love. Without all of this, I would have never achieved my dreams.

I bestow this book to my daughters, Danielle, Ashley, and Lindsey. This is the story of being your mom. Thank you for your willingness to open up our private stories to others so they grow as parents, too. I have told you many of these stories over and over. Some stories touched a nerve so I had to tread lightly, but life as a mom is like that sometimes. When you are moms, I want you all to know that I felt those same feelings, too. I want you to have these stories with you, whether I am across town, across the country, or no longer on this earth with you. I hope you'll enjoy reading this as much as I have loved being your mom.

Love,
Mommy

Contents

Section I: The Parent Team

CHAPTER 1: THE ROAD TO BECOME PARENTS — 1
    Anticipation — 3

CHAPTER 2: THE PARENT DEFENSE — 13
    Double Team Defense — 13
    Man-to-Man Defense — 22
    Zone Defense — 28

CHAPTER 3: THE PARENT OFFENSE — 37
    Give and Go Offense: Bedtime Routine — 37
    Star Player: Special Day — 41
    Daddy's the Coach: Daddy Time — 44
    Recovery: Needing Time to Recharge — 49

Section II: Mom as a Career

CHAPTER 4: FEELING LIKE AN INTERN — 59
    Orientation Day: Bonding Time — 59
    Where are the Instructions? — 65
    Group Projects: Sharing or Taking Turns — 69
    Trust Yourself — 78

CHAPTER 5: FULL TIME MOM ... 89
- My Title ... 90
- Coworkers and Training ... 92
- Job Searching ... 95
- Job Transfer ... 96
- My Work Routine ... 101
- Weekends ... 106
- Commuting: Car Rides ... 109
- Promotion: Time for a Real Job ... 113

CHAPTER 6: MY ROLE AS A MANGER ... 119
- Opposite Projects ... 120
- Juggling Projects: Every Child is Unique ... 121
- To Do List ... 127
- Controlling Your Attitude ... 128
- Integrity ... 131
- Adopting to the Challenge ... 135
- Equal but Different ... 143

CHAPTER 7: PROJECT TESTING ... 151
- Trial and Error: Being in Public ... 151
- Collaboration ... 157
- Report to the Boss ... 162
- The Value of Education ... 168
- Engaged Audience ... 175
- Sharing our Mission: Faith ... 177

Contents

Section III: Working Myself Out of a Job

CHAPTER 8: LETTING HER DO IT — 189
- At the Table — 189
- Getting Dressed — 196
- Mommy Fix It — 204

CHAPTER 9: ALLOWING INDEPENDENCE — 209
- Big Girl Bed — 209
- Stop Nagging — 224
- Staying Home Alone — 230

CHAPTER 10: DELEGATING DECISIONS — 237
- All Done — 237
- Wear That! — 242
- Friend Time — 250
- Dictator Turned Advisor — 269

CHAPTER 11: LETTING GO — 287
- Now What? — 287
- Bite my Tongue — 300
- No Longer Teenagers — 307

References — 313

Preface

Dan has been—and continues to be—an amazing father and partner in our role as parents. However, as I started to write our stories as parents, it was too confusing to sometimes say 'we' when we were parenting together and sometimes say 'I' when he was at work. Because of this, there are stories told as if they were only done by ME, but really Dan was always very much involved. If he wasn't there at the moment something happened, he was there later, to listen to me talk about what happened and why I did what I did in that situation. He listened without judgment. He guided and suggested the best way for us to continue. We have truly been a parenting team and we have learned and grown together.

Dan was a pioneer dad because he was pushed to be more involved with childcare than the generation before him. And he continues to do that with joy, love, and support.

So yes, this book is written from my perspective. I admit to taking credit for doing things that we did together. If Dan wants more credit, he may have to write his own book!

As a busy mom, I would often call one of my girls the wrong name. This happened so many times that Ashley said her name was, "Dalshey."

I will share a little secret to help you keep them straight, even if I couldn't. **'DAL'** is their birth order: Danielle, Ashley, and Lindsey.

Section I:
THE PARENT TEAM

Chapter 1:
The Road to Become Parents

The instant that Danielle, our baby girl, was placed in my arms on my chest, I felt a combination of relief that she was out of me and an intense love. A parent's love is different than any other kind of love. It's a deep, intense love that burns to the core of your own existence.

As I struggled with the pain after birth, I looked up. I saw my husband holding our new daughter. I found just enough strength to finish the birthing process and ask for the camera. I had to take a picture of Dan holding Danielle and capture the look in his eyes as he looked down at her. I knew I wanted to remember this moment forever. After I snapped the photo, Dan walked over and we cuddled

Dan holding newborn Danielle

Danielle, our new baby girl, together. I realized that the love we had shared as husband and wife was now at a higher level, too. Tears ran down my cheeks. As I looked up, I saw tears in Dan's eyes, too. We were now parents. Finally.

❖ ❖ ❖

As I was left alone to rest, I recalled the long road to get here. Growing up, I had always believed I would be a mother. It was just the way it was. In the *'old days'* when I was a child, girls didn't really think about not becoming mothers. It is just what every woman did. The big decision for my generation was to be able to determine *when* to have our children, but not many thought about never having them. In my middle twenties, I started to realize that women *did* have the option of not becoming mothers. I supported my best friend, Jean, as she made the decision to never have a child of her own, as that was what was right for her. And, at that same time, I realized that I *did* want to be a mom. Our generation now had the choice, but *my choice was to be a mom*.

    I thought I had a perfect plan. I was a High School Home Economics teacher, but at that time, I remained single, as I'd had a few relationships that were *not* with Mr. Right. Timing for this marriage thing was taking longer than I had anticipated. So, instead, I decided to pursue a different career dream. I got my Master's degree and became a 4-H & Youth Extension Agent. It was a position that let me stretch my wings as I developed adult volunteers and led educational programs to prepare young people with life skills to step up to the challenges of adulthood. I was totally happy with what I was doing and who I was. That is, until I turned 30 years old. I was still single, and my childbearing years were reaching the later window of opportunity (at least that is how I felt). I started to worry whether I would ever become a mother, and I struggled with that thought. I decided to table the worry for a few more years and make a decision in five years: if I was still single at 35, I would become a mom on my own. I even shared this idea with Jean that if my relationship status didn't change in the next five years, we would be discussing me becoming a single mom. She protested the idea, but I stopped her to point out that we had a few more years before we even had this debate, but we never revisited the conversation. By my next birthday, I was engaged, and Dan and I were married just after I turned 31 years old.

Anticipation

As Dan and I started our married life together, we discussed our plan to become parents. After a year of marriage, we started considering the perfect time to have a child. We believed it was our decision, and we wanted it to be the best timing as possible. Finally, that time came. We understood that we might not get pregnant that first month, but we were sure that it would happen in a short time.

Our Engagement

With nine exciting months of pregnancy, we would be parents in about a year . . . or so we thought.

The first months proved to become an every-month-disappointment. We both agreed we should try for a year before we saw a doctor, but that seemed like forever to me. After seven disheartening months, I couldn't wait any longer and made a doctor's appointment, where I shared how we were trying to conceive a child and how we were saddened that I wasn't pregnant yet. I wanted to know how long we had to wait before we searched for answers. My doctor was very understanding and pointed out that if we were already disappointed each month, there was no need to wait. We could do some simple things right away to determine what could be causing the delay.

Infertility is as complex as putting together a puzzle for which you've only glimpsed the box from afar. First, together with our doctor, we put together the outside pieces of the puzzle, which, for infertility, meant running the simple tests and ruling out the most common causes. One of them was checking Dan's sperm count and health. He was fine and had no problems. I had to check my temperature daily to see if my cycle was normal, and, it, too, followed a healthy pattern.

At this point, the outside of our infertility puzzle was together, yet we still had no answers. The next step–just as it is in any puzzle– was to fill it in with the pieces that had the biggest images on them. In the infertility puzzle, it was clear the problem was with my body; Dan's body was fine. I quickly apologized for being the problem and he pointed out that it was my body, not me as a person. At one point we thought we had found and fixed the problem, but we soon discovered I had yet another issue. This was turning out to be a difficult puzzle.

With a puzzle, if you get stuck, you look at the box; you ask for help, and sometimes you walk away. In our infertility struggle, we had many tests done, which led to more waiting for results and a restart of my cycle. Then I had minor surgery, but still . . . the puzzle was not solved.

Emotions ran strong. It was easy for me to take the blame since Dan was fine. Since the problem was with my body, I often wondered if he would leave me so he could be a dad. Or I would consider if I should let him go so he could be a dad. The best thing I did was share these thoughts with Dan. Each time I would tell him that I felt it was my fault, he would say, "No, we are in this together. We are married and take the good and bad together."

> *As the guilt bug bites, be sure to share your feelings with your mate.*

And even still, the monthly disappointment continued. As the end of my cycle would draw near, I would hold my breath as I walked into the bathroom, as each time I had to be prepared for disappointment. I am sure Dan had to prepare himself also for what seemed like a broken record of the sad news: "We weren't pregnant."

It was hard not to blame God. I also wondered if it

was a delayed answer to my prayers from years earlier when I prayed that I wouldn't get pregnant. Did God listen to me *too* well? Even in the midst of blaming God, I would still look to him to give me peace and patience. Praying over and over to God was the only way for me to finally fall asleep some nights.

Of course there were times our love life was more sex than it was lovemaking. There were just times we just *had* to do it because I was either ovulating or we had to prepare for some test. It was embarrassing to go to the doctor within four hours of sex to test the reaction of my body to Dan's sperm. There were countless days where I'd feel like everyone knew I was a failure, even through Dan's support and comfort that we would keep working to solve this infertility puzzle.

Finally, another cause was identified and the solution was as simple as a drug treatment. This seemed so simple that a drug I would take for five days would be the solution after seven additional months of delay, for a total of 14 months and counting. I opened up the pill container and looked at the five-day prescription of this tiny drug and thought, *Seriously . . . is it possible that it could really be this simple*?

After I took the drug and just before the timing would be perfect, I fell and badly sprained my ankle. I couldn't even walk on it. At first we thought we would have to wait yet *another* month and pay for another round of the drug treatment. But the determination to become parents was stronger than the pain in my ankle as we tried to conceive our child. We had no true hope that this time would be any different than the other fifteen months we tried. We joked about how funny it would be that it took having my foot on a pillow during sex for it to work! But I was happy we were still able to find humor in the middle of this puzzle.

When we couldn't wait any longer, Dan stopped to pick up an at-home pregnancy test. (I was still on crutches for my ankle.) It was time again to try a test, so the next morning, I took the test and I saw a plus sign on the stick. I had never seen that on any of the other tests we had taken. I couldn't believe it was true. I limped back to bed with tears in my eyes and told Dan I was pregnant. We both cried with nervous joy. We were in disbelief. Was this another cruel joke? We still were not sure.

With that added hope, we found a little more patience and waited another couple of weeks. Then I had a test done in the doctor's office.

It was true . . . I was pregnant. Our first baby was going to be born at the worst possible time of the year for both Dan and my careers, but we were both overjoyed. We learned timing wasn't important.

Becoming parents was what it was all about.

Each month was filled with joy and excitement instead of the fear and dread that had become a reoccurring theme in our lives. The moment I heard our baby's heartbeat, I finally let myself believe it was real. My eyes filled with tears that spilled out down my face as I lay there listening to the swooshing sound of the heartbeat of our baby. As our baby grew, I soon felt movement inside of me. Finally, I was able to get an ultrasound of our baby. Dan and I were so excited, but we didn't want to know the sex of the child. After all we had been through to conceive, we only wanted to focus on having a healthy baby. The ultrasound showed that the baby was in fact very healthy, was the perfect size, and was sucking its thumb. Once again, joyful tears filled my eyes.

I continued to have a very happy, healthy pregnancy. After spending over a year and a half doubting if this day would ever come, my perspective on how the pregnancy felt was rooted in gratitude. I found joy in the process and the reality of becoming a mom. Dan talked to my belly and the baby would kick his hand as he did so, letting us know that the baby recognized his voice.

As I got larger, I had to get up during the night and early in the morning. I took notice that I was up almost every night at 2:00 a.m. I started to wonder if that meant that I would be up feeding our baby at that time. I always woke up early in the morning and would often have trouble getting back to sleep. Would that really mean this baby was going to grow into an early bird? Anticipation of life with a newborn was building.

I found out that when you have a pregnant belly, many people think that your stomach is now public property. I was shocked at the number of people that would walk up to me and brazenly touch my stomach. Most of the time it was family or close friends, but none of these people had ever touched my stomach before. Many of them I had never even hugged before, so why would it suddenly be acceptable for them to touch my stomach? To this day, I still do not understand that concept. I had a really hard time when strangers would ask if they could touch my stomach. This was still part of my body! I finally decided that I would think of my stomach as my baby, so when these people would ask if they could touch my stomach as they were reaching out to it, I responded as I would if they were about to hold my baby. I would not let a stranger hold my baby, so I didn't let a stranger touch my stomach. If it was a family member or friend I would love to have hold my new baby, I would allow them to touch my stomach. It was good practice for drawing these kinds of boundaries, but I was still not prepared to have my pregnant body feel so public.

Not only did people want to touch me, but it seemed like every woman had advice or a story to tell. I got more unsolicited advice than anyone should have to listen to. Perhaps it was my payback since I always give advice (thus the purpose of this book). But through that process, I learned how to half listen, be in a hurry at times and when needed, or excuse myself by saying, "I am not ready to hear that."

However, once in a while I heard very helpful advice. A fear I had (like many pregnant women do) was what happens if my water breaks? Being nine months pregnant and having the baby kick my bladder, I had already had the experience of running/waddling to a bathroom as I started to pee. A grocery store clerk told me, "If your water breaks here, just stand still," she insisted. "Please just stand still. It is much easier to clean up one puddle than a river that goes all the way down the aisle and out the door."

Believe it or not, that put my mind at ease. I had been in many grocery stores when someone dropped something, it broke, and there was the *'clean up on aisle number five'* announcement. So I realized my water breaking in the middle of a store would not be the first— or last— spill they would have. The other piece of advice on this subject was to put a garbage bag under your mattress pad on your bed. It will save your mattress from getting wet if your water breaks while you are in bed. I loved this idea until it was July and sleeping on plastic made me feel like I was overheating. But nevertheless, I did it for the sake of our mattress.

My due date was the first day of my job's biggest annual event. Dan was finishing up his Doctorate and even scheduled his dissertation defense on our due date. He figured that no one actually delivers on their due date, so it would be the best date. When he shared that news with me, I had a hormonal fit. I just knew the baby would be born that day. Dan knew not to reason with a pregnant wife, so he changed his dissertation date to one week later.

I was right.

At 2:00 a.m. on our due date, my water broke. I stayed in bed on the plastic and didn't jump out of bed and have a river to the bathroom. (The advice I never asked for did help.) And nineteen hours later, Danielle, our first little girl, was born.

Rearview Mirror of The Road to Become Parents

Looking back, I realize that by not getting married until I was 31 years old and with our infertility problems, I treasured my role as a mom. I had feared I would never be a mother. That fear guided all of my decisions as a parent.

I understand that our infertility problems were such a short time in our life. But as we were living it, it consumed us and seemed to last forever. I now know our problems were not as complex as many others I have talked to throughout the years. My heart goes out to everyone who struggles with infertility, especially those who will never be able to have children.

As I think back to the very first moment I held my little girl, my eyes once again fill with tears. I now know it's not hormones; it is the reaction I have to everything! From the moment I became pregnant to the day I die, tears will fill my eyes for the silliest things. It's a mom's right!

Chapter 2:
The Parent Defense

Dan and I were parents, and in just a few days, we headed home. Back at our apartment, Dan hauled in all of the stuff from the hospital. I laid baby Danielle in her new bassinet. Dan looked up at me and said, "Now what?"

Now, we were parents. The new chapter of our life had started. Fear and love were mixed together as we looked down at Danielle. Those same emotions would continue to find their way back into our hearts many times as parents.

Double Team Defense

Dan and I are total opposites. So much so that we don't enjoy any of the same music or TV shows. But one thing we can enjoy together is watching sports: we love to watch football, baseball, and basketball together.

Because of this affinity, it became clear to us early on that Dan and I were a parent team. Like a basketball team's defense, we had the *'double team'* strategy. There were two of us and only one child. But as new parents we had to learn as much as possible. Dan and I learned how to care for our daughter together. As Dan changed her for the first time, I tried to let him do what he had learned and not teach him what I thought we learned. To help me stay quiet and not give advice (which is very hard for me), I kept the image of Dan holding our new baby girl in my head—the photo I took right after labor. That image helped me remember that Danielle was just as much his baby as she was mine. He wanted to learn to be a part of her life, as did I. We were both new parents, learning together.

We were both able to be home with Danielle during that first month. Dan completed his dissertation defense one week after Danielle's birth and finished up the last details to complete his degree. We were able to take turns parenting and have individual time to get things done or just sleep. Since I was breastfeeding, I had the task of feeding her, which only left burping and changing for Dan. I realized how getting most of the diaper duty didn't seem fair for Dan, so I tried to hand her off as soon as I was done feeding her. That way he could do the last burping, hold her, and comfort her to sleep. Sometimes I still wanted to be touching my newborn, but I would look at the two of them and it filled my heart with so much love that it was easy to share. I'd sit right next to Dan so all of us were a part of this new family. Occasionally, I enjoyed a peaceful shower or a nap. Double team coverage was very nice.

We had decided I would stay at home with Danielle and not return to work. For me, that was an easy decision because I already achieved two of my career dreams, being a high school teacher *and* becoming a 4-H & Youth Agent in my home county. I looked at motherhood

The Parent Defense

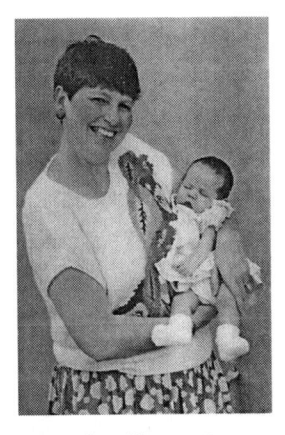

I'm finally a Mom

as my next career decision.

Financially, the decision was easy for us. I had been a professional when Dan was a research assistant attending graduate school. Now that he had finished his degree, he would be starting a professional career. We needed to move for his employment, so I would have had to leave my job anyway. The timing that we thought wasn't the best ended up working out perfectly for us.

The first thing Dan desired was for Danielle to recognize her daddy. I think being left out of feeding and cuddle time is hard for new dads . . . at least it was for Dan. Danielle would stick out her tongue, like babies do, and Dan would stick his tongue out back at her and give her a big hug. Then Danielle would do it back and Dan would imitate her: a new game began. Each time Dan would hold Danielle, she would stick out her tongue and Dan would copy her and hug her. After awhile, Danielle would do it when Dan would pick her up from a nap or say goodbye to her. Dan was convinced Danielle recognized her daddy and that she was saying hi and bye to him with her tongue. I was a little doubtful, so I tried it with Danielle as I picked her up from a nap. She didn't stick out her tongue or imitate me when I did it. It wasn't our game; it was her daddy's game. My feelings were hurt. I had to remind myself that I was part of the Parent Team and this was *their* thing. So each time baby Danielle would see or hear her daddy, she would stick out her tongue. He was so excited that she recognized him.

> *It's important for the baby to bond with Daddy.*

Our family went from a small two-bedroom apartment in southern Wisconsin to our new three-bedroom house in Rochester, Minnesota. I was so excited to move into our new house, and I looked forward to getting us all moved in. I didn't realize how much of my time and energy was taken up with the care of a child. I remember Dan coming home at the end of the first week to find me in tears. "I just want to have my kitchen," I cried.

He tried to find a calm way to offer to help and work together to get it done. I burst into tears, so he just held me until I was done. Then he asked, "How about we just do one box at a time?"

Before I could object, he opened a box and started unwrapping. He pointed out he would just unwrap, while I put things exactly where I wanted them. We worked for about an hour until Danielle woke up. We took a break to feed her and then continued with our boxes in the kitchen. We continued going back and forth until all the kitchen boxes were unpacked. We went to bed late that night, but I was a much happier mommy.

I knew I was adjusting to my new role as a mom, a

new house, and a new town. But I never thought that a six-week-old baby would know any different . . . but the first few days were a struggle. Danielle was turning into a cranky baby. Of course, I thought it was just a new stage. I tried walking her, feeding her, changing her, rocking her, and finally passing her to Dan to repeat all of the above. Nothing seemed to work. Dan thought it might be the move, but I figured she couldn't know the difference. How could a six-week-old baby know any different? I thought she was just picking up on my stress. So I tried to relax and repeat all of the above again. It just didn't work. Out of total frustration I just laid her in her bassinet that was sitting in the dining room and walked away to calm down. Within a few moments, she stopped crying. Dan walked over to look at her. She was looking up at the chair rail in the dining room, quietly staring. I asked, "What is she looking at?"

"The chair rail," Dan answered just as he remembered. "In our apartment there was a dark shelf just above her changing table. The chair rail looked like the shelf above her old changing table. She had missed her home, but now she found it again." Danielle was content. I realized that as a mom, I wouldn't know all of the answers. There were times it would take both of us to figure things out.

> *Accept that as a mom, you don't know all the answers.*

With Dan now working full time, we struggled to find a way to keep his strong connection with Danielle. I realized that one of the most awake and active times for a baby was bath time. So I asked him about moving bath time to the evening instead of me doing it in the morning. It could be something he did with her every day. Dan was willing to give it a try, but he had never given a baby a bath before, so this time I taught him my method. Whenever I was nervous as a new mom, I sang; it helped me stay calm. So I had started a bath song. I taught Dan my silly song and showed him how I washed each part of the body as I sang the song. "Rubby dubby dubby the tummy, the tummy. Rubby dubby dubby the arms, the arms. Rubby dubby dubby the back, the back. Rubby dubby dubby the legs, the legs. Rubby dubby dubby the butt, the butt."

Even though Dan is not a singer, he learned the silly song and sang it every night at bath time. Dad and Danielle now had a special time every night.

Just when I thought I had a parent double team play book that worked, Danielle changed. There were times when all Danielle wanted was her mommy, and daddy wouldn't do. At first I thought I could just teach Dan my technique, but that didn't work. It wasn't until Danielle was comforted by Dan and wouldn't let me comfort her did I realize that it wasn't a technique. Danielle was demanding a certain parent at a certain time. My feelings were hurt! I again had to remind myself that Dan and I were a parent team.

> *It's all about the baby, not about your feelings.*

It didn't matter who was making Danielle happy, just that she was happy. So I started using phrases to help me cope with my hurt feelings: *'daddy fix it'* and *'mommy's touch'*. There were still times we tried to teach each other how to do it our way, and had to keep re-learning that what worked for one didn't work for the other. Danielle wanted *'daddy fix it'* and I had to let him do it. Of course there were times my feelings would still get hurt. I would sometimes think I was a failure as a mom, and I would have to remind myself to be a good team player.

We decided to visit my longtime friend, Jean, and her husband Dick, for our anniversary, traveling almost 500 miles one way. Taking our first trip as parents with one child was not as simple as I thought it would be. Just packing to take the trip was a challenge. I was reminded that we were in a new chapter in our lives and I couldn't just throw a few clothes into a suitcase. Thank goodness I remembered to pack extra clothes for us, and not just for Danielle, since most of the accidents ended up on our clothes! I had to pack about three times the stuff. To accomplish the task of packing, I packed while Dan took care of Danielle . . . the great double team approach.

Timing of the trip was completely based around Danielle's schedule, so Dan worked a half a day on our departure day. That way Danielle could have an active morning and I would quickly load the stuff into the car during her morning nap. We timed it so I was just finishing feeding Danielle her lunch as Dan walked into the house. Dan grabbed a sandwich as I changed Danielle and put her into her car seat. We hadn't driven long before Danielle had fallen asleep for her afternoon nap. That gave us about 2 hours on the road before she even woke up. We were able to stop for supper to feed her and give her time to move around before we put her back into her car seat for a couple more hours on the road. We thought we were making a wise decision to stop at her bedtime to put her to sleep in a hotel to break up the 12-hour trip. We found out our nine-month-old didn't like her new portable crib or to be laid down in a strange room. We felt so concerned about how loud her cry was to our hotel room neighbors. We tried everything to stop her. It seemed like none of us got much sleep that night.

Traveling the next morning was difficult with all of us having little sleep. Finally, after a few extra stops, Danielle fell asleep and we were able make it to our Akron, Ohio destination. We had a great time visiting friends. We found putting Danielle to bed in their house was so much easier than the hotel. At first I wasn't sure why, but then I realized that when we put her in her portable crib at their house, we walked out of the bedroom. In the hotel room, we stayed in the room with her, of course. She wasn't used to us staying in her room when she went to sleep so she didn't think it was time to go to sleep.

It worked out great to have one parent take care of Danielle while the other had uninterrupted time to talk to our friends. Keeping her on her routine and having quiet time after she was in bed worked out perfectly. We also learned that it was not as relaxing to go out to a restaurant at night and keep Danielle up past her bedtime. We grew and accepted our new chapter in our life: parenthood.

Since we were visiting friends who didn't have children, we decided to take a one-day excursion on our own. We went to Sea World for a relaxing day as a family and I think it gave our friends some needed quiet time since they weren't used to having a baby around 24/7. We had planned to do more activities that day, but realized that Danielle had done enough after being at Sea World. So once again, we learned to adjust to being parents and did not just focus on our own schedule, but on Danielle's.

The return trip started out as it began. We left right after lunch so Danielle was well fed and ready for her afternoon nap. We stopped for supper, but kept driving afterwards to let Danielle fall asleep in her car seat. She stayed asleep when we had a quick rest stop and switched drivers a couple of times. Once at home, she easily fell back to sleep in her own bed. We had learned how to double-team a family trip.

> *A trip with a baby is all about timing. Their timing! You drive when they are sleeping, stop for gas and food when they need to eat. And you never take a rest stop when you need it and the baby is sleeping!*

Man-to-Man Defense

We knew that we didn't want just one child, but I was **old**, and it had taken us awhile to have the first, so we decided to leave it in God's hands. To our surprise, God didn't want us to wait. I found out I was expecting our second child on my 35th birthday when Danielle was just six months old! I was pregnant, again. We were going to have two children in less than a year and a half.

Thank goodness this pregnancy was just as easy for me as the first. I listened to the advice of others and took a nap when Danielle took a nap. The hardest time for me was when I was in the last month of pregnancy. Danielle was getting more mobile and I was more tired. Also, Danielle seemed to get really clingy and wanted to sit on my lap. There just wasn't enough room on my lap anymore and I felt like she was getting pushed away. I don't know if that is what she felt, but in my hormonal state that is how *I* felt, so I made up a poem for us to say together.

"When Mommy has another baby, her love doesn't get smaller." I would move my hands together. "No, Mommy's love grows bigger and bigger," and I'd spread my arms far apart. "Her love will get this big," I reached my arms as far as they could reach. "And that love will wrap all around you," I'd say as I grabbed her into a big hug.

"More . . . more," Danielle would say. And I would do it over and over again. It made us both feel better.

Just like with our first child, we didn't want to know the sex of our next baby. I was convinced it would be a boy, but Dan always thought it would be a girl. With Danielle so young, we needed another crib, so we picked one up at a garage sale and moved Danielle out of the nursery and into the other bedroom, which I called the big girls' room (since I believed the nursery would now be the boy's room). We were ready for the change in our defense.

Just three days before my due date, our second daughter, Ashley, was born. (Yes, Dan was right!)

As parents, we had to move from the double team defense to a man-to-man coverage. With man-to-man coverage, you don't have time to sit on the bench. You are always in the game. The constant question was, 'Which one do you want?' There seemed to be the constant handoff. I would pass one child off with my right hand as I reached for the other girl with my left hand. We quickly fell into a new pattern. I would breastfeed Ashley as Dan played with Danielle. It was easy for me to continue with Ashley to burp her and hold her as Danielle loved playing with her daddy, and I loved to watch Danielle's relationship with her daddy grow stronger.

Then one day, Dan pointed out how he really missed getting a chance to get to know baby Ashley like he had

Holding newborn Ashley

Danielle. He felt like he wasn't getting a chance to bond with her. His news wasn't surprising to me, as Dan was able to take a month off when Danielle was a baby, and now he was working full time. He only had evenings and weekends to be around the girls, but I felt bad that he was missing out on bonding with Ashley, so I decided to take a mom and toddler swimming class with Danielle one night a week which would give Dan time to be with Ashley, feed her, rock her, and put her to bed while I was gone. It would give Danielle time to be the only child with Mommy one night a week.

Things didn't go as smoothly as I thought they would. Without even realizing it, I had always breastfed Ashley and now she was refusing to take a bottle. Dan tried to hold her close to his bare chest to help her feel flesh like mommy as he gave her the bottle. He tried every bottle type and nipple, but nothing seemed to work. Dan ended up just comforting her until I got back to breastfeed her. To Dan's credit, he didn't tell me how much she resisted, or how crabby she was, until months later. He just said she didn't eat much, and that I may want to feed her. Ashley was determined to not drink from a bottle again, and she didn't.

Danielle loved having time to go swimming with Mommy, but she was not happy when Dan held baby Ashley. Each time, Danielle would cry, "My daddy!"

That's when I realized the pattern into which we had fallen. I would take care of Ashley with the breastfeeding, burping, and holding while Dan was busy with Danielle. We had successfully switched to man-to-man coverage, but we never switched girls. I took care of baby Ashley and when Dan was home, he took care of Danielle. We were not doing the hand off; we were just playing man-to-man coverage.

I had to start to focus on Dan taking baby Ashley whenever she was done eating. That became a big adjustment for 18-month-old Danielle. She didn't like sharing her favorite toy, *her daddy*. At first I pointed out that Dan was Ashley's daddy, too, but that made things worse. Then I pointed out how she was the big sister and she could hold baby Ashley. But that ended with, "All done."

I quickly learned that her *'all done'* was not just to holding her sister. She was all done with *being* a big sister. I had to change my focus.

> *Be aware of what your toddler is trying to tell you.*

I needed to think about what I could give Danielle, instead of what we were taking away from her. We were taking away her daddy, but I was focusing on her. So I expanded *'mommy's touch'* to start to have *'mommy time.'* Danielle and I would play the piano together, have a tea party, read a book, or do a craft. That would be *'mommy time.'* Of course, she was still adjusting to sharing her daddy, so sometimes she would demand, "No mommy time. I want daddy!"

When that would happen, we'd default to a defensive hand-off where I would take Ashley and Dan would take Danielle . . . and I had to develop a thick skin. It was hard to hear my daughter didn't want me, especially with post-pregnancy hormones happening. But I tried to focus on the positive, even through the tears. Dan desired to have that great relationship with his daughters and they needed it, too. I had to keep working on being a parent team player!

There were times we needed to force a parent pass off. I would be at the end of my rope, losing my temper, or over reacting. Dan would step in and take over. Of course, I would not handle it well and would stomp off in my own little temper tantrum. Then one night, I heard Dan trying to rush bath time. He was yelling at the girls for being silly. I thought it was strange since many nights he *started* the silliness. I realized he was not feeling like himself, so I stepped in and told him I would finish the baths for him. He said, "Fine," and walked out.

He reacted much better than I usually did, but I realized his feelings were hurt. So after the girls were in bed that night, we talked. I explained what I heard and he got defensive. I went on to explain about the times when I was losing my temper and he stepped in. He was able to see that I needed him to step in those times and perhaps he needed me to step in this time. We started to figure out that sometimes we needed to take a pass and have the other parent step in.

Realize it's easier to see the mistakes others make, but perhaps are they a reflection of your own?

However, the person needing the pass didn't always realize it. We needed a way to communicate that quickly and kindly so the other parent didn't get so defensive. Then I realized it was like tag team wrestling. (Although I hadn't watched wrestling since I was little and watched it with my grandpa, the concept stuck in my head.) When one of the wrestlers is getting tired or beat up, they tag the other and they switch places. That is what we needed to do. So we decided to use the word, 'tag'.

When I would start to over react and yell, Dan would say, 'tag,' as he stepped in. I was able to curb my feelings a little better and sometimes we could even learn from each other. As we got used to this concept, we were even able to ask for a 'tag', or ask if a 'tag' was needed. This became a great advantage of being a parenting team.

Finally, Dan and I had adjusted to the man-to-man coverage. It seemed like Danielle had forgotten she had been an only child. She was enjoying her mommy time *and* her daddy time. The phrase *'Daddy Fix It'* had changed to be *'Daddy Time'* to include more fun times together, instead of just Dan caring for Danielle. She had also adjusted to having baby Ashley around. She loved to lay down on the floor with Ashley and bring her toys. When Ashley was napping, Danielle would ask, "Where Hiya?"

I had no idea what she was saying, but over time it became obvious that was the name she had given Ashley. Then one night I was holding Ashley, Dan came in with Danielle and said to Danielle, "Say hi to baby Ashley."

"That's it," I yelled. "That is what Danielle is saying, say hi to your sister, has been shorten to Hiya."

"Hiya," Danielle said and smiled.

Zone Defense

As I was packing up baby clothes that Ashley had outgrown, I started to wonder if I was packing them up for the last time. Were we going to be a family of four and have just two children? Were we ever going to have our boy? I think it was hormones, but I wanted to know if we were going to have more children. I realized that it was a crazy subject to bring up to Dan when we had two children under the age of two, but when we left the girls with their grandparents for a long weekend on our fifth anniversary, I decided it was time to ask. (I tend to bring up big subjects on road trips. Maybe it's because Dan is stuck in the car and can't walk away.)

When I brought up the subject, Dan had this feeling that I was already pregnant. I thought he was crazy. Just because we had celebrated our love for each other without protection at the wrong time didn't mean I would really get pregnant, and especially not after all the effort we had gone through to conceive the first time. I knew it was possible, but I believed very improbable. I continued to force the discussion. We decided if Dan was right and I was currently pregnant then we would have one more child. All three children would be close in age. If I was right and I wasn't pregnant, we would wait a couple of years, and then have two more children also close together like the first two. Dan didn't want the third child to feel left out with the first two being so close in age. I loved the plan. I wanted at least one more baby.

> *Compromise is as important in parenting as it is in marriage.*

Dan was right; I was pregnant. Adjusting to the idea of having a third child seemed easy and exciting. I enjoyed every moment of the pregnancy because I knew it would be my last. However, I had more morning sickness, was so tired, and with two toddlers, this pregnancy was anything but easy. I continued my prayer to God about my fear of having twins. Dan has twin brothers, his mother is a twin, and my grandmother was a twin. I figured we were destined to have twins. So during each pregnancy I prayed to be spared twins.

"Just not my first child," I had prayed.

Then, "Not with having another baby when the first was under 15 months old."

And this time it was: "Not with two children under three years old! Please, oh please, don't give me more than one!"

I had a constant fear that I would have twins. As I struggled with this pregnancy and two toddlers, I wasn't sure I was going to be able to handle one infant. Certainly I couldn't handle two.

Dan was happy being a father of girls and even hoped this one was a girl. He wasn't sure he would be a good dad to a boy, but I really wanted one boy. I needed to know ahead of time so I could adjust just in case. So we decided to find out the sex of this child.

Once again, Dan was right; we were having a girl. Of course I was disappointed, but I was very glad to not be having twins, and that this was another healthy child. Most importantly, I was happy to be able to adjust before she was born.

During this pregnancy, as Ashley turned one, she decided to focus on her verbal skills instead of her physical skills. Since she wasn't walking yet and I was five months pregnant, I was not excited about this. Kids seem to focus on one thing at a time and she decided to be an early talker and a slow walker. I learned to spend a great deal of time on the floor. It was easier to hug them and play with them than pick them up to sit with me on the couch. Then the girls were exposed to chickenpox when I was in the last trimester. Thank goodness, Lindsey was tucked safely inside of me during that time.

With all of this going on, I was the one that needed to be reminded of Mommy's love. I would say this poem to each of the girls or even both of them together. "When Mommy has another baby, her love doesn't get smaller," I would move my hands closer together. "No, Mommy's love grows bigger and bigger," I'd say as I spread my arms far apart. "Her love gets this big," and I reached my arms as far as they could reach. "And my love wraps all around you," as I grabbed them into a big hug.

We were experienced parents and thought we were ready for our third child. But before she was even born, we were proven wrong. It started with having early labor, which meant I had to drink lots of water and lay down. That lasted off and on for a week. Then we went to the hospital with false labor. We found out the only thing more disappointing than false labor was to get the bill while we were still pregnant. Finally, a week over due and the fourth time in the hospital, we had our third girl, Lindsey. I was so excited to finally hold her that I was not at all disappointed that I didn't have a boy. She was the perfect child to complete our family.

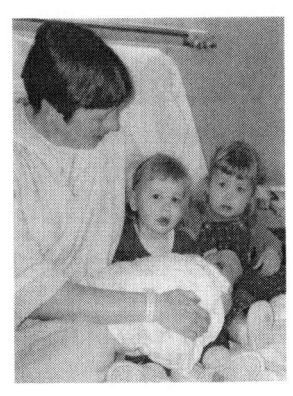

God did answer my prayer in that we didn't have twins, but we did have three little girls. It wasn't until years later when I looked at this picture of me in the hospital with all three girls did I realize that I was truly crazy.

I think Dan always wondered how we were going to do it. Danielle, at 30 months old, was in the middle of her terrible twos and Ashley, at 16 months, had just learned to walk. Even with a newborn, I was confident. We could do it; we were experienced parents. We had figured out 'mommy time' *and* 'daddy time.' We thought we were ready and the adjustment to the third child should be easy. We were wrong!

Crazy Mom with three girls in 30 months!

We hadn't realized that you can't play man-to-man defense with three children and two parents. We now had to switch to zone defense.

We were definitely reacting to them. *They* determined who got the attention. The one who was the loudest got one-on-one time with a parent. While the other two girls got zone defense from the other parent. We remembered to be sure Dan had time with the baby, so when he got home from work I would hand him baby Lindsey so he would have 'daddy time' with her. I would take care of the other two until it was time for Lindsey to eat. Then we would switch and I would breastfeed Lindsey and the other two would have their 'daddy time.' The older two seemed to always get team coverage, but that was the best we could do. Whenever we could sneak in some individual time for them we did, like when baby Lindsey napped or went to bed early.

Bath time was still a daddy job, even as we added to our family. But now with three little girls under the age of three, it took both of us to manage bath and bedtime. It started with Dan carrying the older girls up the stairs as he said, "bumpy, bumpy, bump," all the way up. I would help each child get undressed while Dan ran the water for the bathtub. First Danielle— and then Ashley— would run naked from the bedroom down the hall. It was so cute to watch their bare baby butts running and crawling down that hall. Dan would lift them into the tub as I carried Lindsey into the bathroom and set her into the tub. The three girls would play and sing in the tub as Dan washed them up, youngest to oldest.

As soon as Lindsey was finished, I was handed a towel-wrapped baby. I put her into her pajamas, breastfed her, and put her into bed. Meanwhile, the older girls loved having the extra time to play in the tub while Dan finished washing their hair. As I returned to the bathroom, Dan would lift Ashley out of the tub and into my arms as I wrapped *her* in a towel. I carried her to the big girls' room, dried her off, and put her into her pajamas. At the same time, Dan would wrap Danielle in her towel and send her down the hall on her way to me as he picked up the bath toys and the bathroom. I would help Danielle dry off as she worked to put on her pajamas on her own.

As soon as the girls were ready for bed, they could each pick out one book for story time. I would give them each a kiss and hug, and Dan would read the books to both of the big girls before he tucked them into bed. During story time, I picked up the toys and put everything away, and when Dan would was done reading, we would finally be done with the bedtime routine.

Parenting with zone defense with three little girls took both of us. We basically reacted to their demands. We used our tag team approach. There was really not a chance to take a break with zone defense. Now it was about switching which child we were caring for without the ability to step away. But we coped and it seemed to be working . . . that is until I realized that whoever the loudest child was still received the individual attention, and the other two girls had to share the other parent. Zone defense did work, but we needed an offense. We needed to stop being reactive and start being *pro*active.

In the Rearview Mirror of The Parent Defense

Looking back, I recognize that my emotions were intense. I was feeling such deep love for my new family, but I would flip out over the littlest things. If I didn't know exactly what my baby wanted or needed, I found that I would feel like a failure. The solution was to express my feelings and not try to control them. My emotions had to run their course.

Both of us realized communication was the key to our success as parents. We learned over and over again the importance of taking time to talk so we could adjust our own behaviors to become better parents. I appreciate Dan's willingness to listen to my countless ideas as we sorted out the best defense to deal with the girls. I am thankful it worked out that I was older when I had the girls, so I had already learned how to bite my tongue before responding. This came in handy each time I wanted to correct his approach, but I will admit there were times I blurted out the 'right' way to do it! It was so important for me to learn to let go and let Dan have a role and responsibility as a parent. It wasn't about the right way; more than one way could be right. It was more essential to share the parenthood role and let Dan be a daddy.

As very busy parents, bath time was just something that had to be done. But with the silly song that Dan continued to sing through the years, it has become a cherished memory. As the girls got older, they started to sing it as they washed themselves. When they were old enough to take their own showers, we would ask them if they washed everything like in the song and it brought a smile to their faces. Just a silly made up song worked for years.

Chapter 3:
The Parent Offense

In a sports team, you need a strong defense, but you will not win a game if you don't have a good offensive. Both sides of the ball are important. As we dealt with the adjustment to parenthood and the adjustment of adding another child almost yearly, we never had a chance to be on the offense. But we were finally done adding to our family. We had lived through the craziness of the first year of life *three times* back to back. We understood our defensive plays, which meant we were reacting to them. It was time to anticipate their moves and react (or *respond,* rather) before they did. It was time to build an offense.

Give and Go Offense: Bedtime Routine

The one thing that was working smoothly was our bath and bedtime routine, but it took up a huge part of our night. When we finished putting the girls to bed, we would return to the other evening chores, finish washing our supper dishes, and picking up the house. By the time we were finished, we were tired and done for the night, too. Then one night we were out later than usual, so we skipped bath time. The bedtime routine worked just fine without the bath and took a lot less time. A light bulb went off. There was not a cardinal rule that toddlers had a bath every night, so we started to do baths *every other* night.

On non-bath nights, I would take the girls up to do the bedtime routine. Dan would work on the other evening chores. When I had finished reading their books, Dan would come up to kiss them goodnight and tuck them in. On bath nights, we would both help with the bath routine, but Dan read to the girls while I worked on the evening chores before returning to say good night. We took turns: sometimes it was Daddy's turn to read and sometimes it was Mommy's turn. Now, all three girls were tucked in for the night by 8:00. The evening chores were done around the same time. We had time as a couple. We had our first offensive play.

And just when I thought we were making some progress, the girls threw a curveball into my plan.

> *Change is the only constant in parenting!*

They would argue that they wanted Daddy to read the books that night, not Mommy. Or they wanted to lie next to Mommy, not next to Danielle. They would complain that they couldn't see the pictures in the book; they didn't want to hear that story, or sometimes they would just cry. I realized what had worked was not working any longer. I kept trying to get it to work, being the adult in the situation, and demanding that they stop fighting and listen. At times, I would put the complaining child to bed without a book, but that never worked, since they would just cry and complain louder so that Dan would get roped in to helping out, which is exactly what the girls wanted: individual time with Daddy!

I needed to figure out a way to get back on the offensive. I started by actually listening to what they were complaining about. They wanted alone time with one parent, and they didn't want to always feel like they were part of a pack. At first I didn't think that was even possible, as we didn't have three parents. But the next day when all three girls were fighting over the dollhouse, I sat down with them to try to teach them to come up with a solution. I explained, "Ashley, you play with this half of the dollhouse. Danielle, you sit over here and play with the other half." I moved her. "Lindsey you take the dollhouse van and play over here," I said as I gave her the van and the mommy toy.

"That won't work. I want all of it," Ashley cried.

"I don't want to share the van," Danielle whined.

"No, I want more," Lindsey yelled.

Oh my goodness, all three of them were crying and screaming at me. I realized I had started a war that was much worse than before I had gotten involved. So I calmly asked, "What do you want to do?"

"Take turns," Ashley said.

"I go second," Danielle offered, and went to play with the farm set. "Do you want to play with me?" she asked Lindsey.

Lindsey threw the van at Ashley, but didn't complain and went to play with the farm. I have no idea if Ashley had the dollhouse first or if Danielle was being her usual, sweet, patient sister and just let her. She was very happy not to have to share with her sister . . . that message was clear.

That night as I began to read their books, Danielle complained. "I don't want that book."

"It's my turn to lay by Mommy," whined Ashley.

"I want Daddy," cried Lindsey.

As I took a deep breath, thinking about my long day of this, it hit me.

"Wait a minute, do you guys want to take turns with Mommy?" At once, they stopped whining and crying to look at me.

"Danielle, you take your book and Ashley you take this book. Both of you go wait on your beds for Mommy. Be quiet and just wait on your bed and then I will come read your book just to you." I paused and looked at their excited faces.

"Really, all by myself," Danielle asked.

"Yep, but you have to wait quietly," I explained. Off they went to their room. I anticipated noise and fighting as I read Lindsey's book, but I heard none. After I kissed Lindsey good night, I quickly ran downstairs and told Dan to come up and say good night to just Lindsey, quickly adding that I would explain what happened later.

When I walked into the big girls' room, they were both lying on their beds looking at their books, waiting. "My turn," Ashley sat up with excitement.

"Exactly," I said. Dan waited outside of their room, and when I finished reading Ashley's book, and got up to sit with Danielle, he came in and quietly kissed Ashley good night.

"Can we do this every night?" Danielle asked after I finished her story. I told her we would check with Daddy and her sisters and see. She smiled, hopeful that she could always have her special time.

When Dan had finished tucking Danielle in, he said, "That was the happiest I have seen those girls go to sleep. What did you do?"

"I just took turns," and I went on to explain how it had unfolded. That was the start of a new bedtime routine. They would each pick their own book and wait on their bed for their turn. Dan or I would go to each bed and read their one book, remember one parent was doing other chores. I was shocked to find that they were very patient waiting for their turns. They would rather have individual time with a parent than share.

Proof that the parent offensive was working was on the nights that Dan worked late. Our bedtime routine was not affected because one parent was doing bedtime on their own already. The girls were used to just one of us putting them to bed and waiting their turn, so when Dan worked late, the girls' routine was not affected. It just meant that I had to do all of the evening chores after they were in bed. We were starting to establish the ability for one of us have time on the bench, like when we were in double coverage, with one child!

Star Player: Special Day

When the girls were two, three, and four years old,

it seemed like they argued about everything. This became very obvious as we were trying to get out of the house one day. As we were trying to walk out the door, they started arguing and pushing each other, fighting over who got to walk out the door first. I lost my cool and yelled.

"STOP IT! We are not going!" It startled the girls into silence.

We came back in the house and sat in the living room as I tried to calm down. The girls were confused, but knew I was mad so they just sat next to me. I was thinking about the stupid arguments of the morning, who had picked the TV show, who held the remote, who got to brush their teeth first, to finally who walked out the door first! My mind was spinning with everything that I had observed, but the girls were still confused; they had no idea what they did wrong. They were just being sisters and fighting over everything.

Danielle asked if I needed a hug.

I said, "Yes, I need a hug, and I am sorry for yelling."

I needed to switch off the defensive and go to offensive. I decided we were going to have a Special Day. I told the girls, "Today is Ashley's special day. So Ashley gets to pick the TV show, hold the remote, get her teeth brushed first, and walk out the door first."

They all were so confused by my list of things. Ashley was smiling because it was her special day, even though she didn't know what that meant. It sounded good. Finally, when I said she got to walk out the door first, I got up and off we went. I went on to explain as we headed to the car. "Tomorrow will be Danielle's special day and then the day after will be Lindsey's special day."

> *Reinforce positive behavior to reduce your child's need to seek attention through negative behavior.*

I waited for them to ask what exactly the special day meant, but they didn't care. It sounded like a special treat, and that's all they needed to know. That night when I explained it to Dan, I told him it was anything they argued over. As the girls headed up to bed, I heard them starting to argue over who was getting their book read first. I yelled up after them, "Whose special day is it?"

"Mine," Ashley said, joyfully.

"I like having special days, too," Dan said, too quiet for any of the girls to hear. As a side note, I never understood why each girl wanted to be first with their book-reading time when that meant they were the first one tucked into bed!

It didn't take long for the arguing to shift to who went second. To make it fair, I went in alphabetical order. If I was going to have to remember this, I had to have a system: Ashley, Danielle, and Lindsey would be the order. I was shocked by how well having a special day took care of so much whining and arguing. Anytime any of the girls fought, we would default to the Special Day rule. Sometimes it was a disadvantage to be first, but it didn't matter. It was their Special Day, so they went first.

Daddy's the Coach: Daddy Time

Dan's job had started to take over his life. He was missing many dinners and even some bedtimes. It just seemed that no matter how hard he tried, he couldn't control the end of his workday, sometimes not getting home until bedtime or even after the girls were asleep. Eventually, I told him to either come home 30 minutes *before* bedtime or *after* they were sound asleep. He was really missing time with the girls, who, at the time, were three, five, and six years old. So he started getting to work 45 minutes later each day in order to have some quality time with the girls every morning that he could count on. Each morning, he would read a chapter of *Little House in the Prairie*[1] to Danielle and soon Ashley would wake up and join in. Many mornings he would finish the chapter just as Lindsey would wake up and want to join in, so he would read one more chapter. That's when our big, old, brown Lazy Boy became 'the reading chair'.

The Reading Chair

Dan had Danielle on one armrest, Ashley on the other armrest, and Lindsey sat right in the middle. It didn't matter that Danielle was learning to read; this was a chapter book and *with Dad*! They loved their special Daddy Time each day. Dan had created a special time in his crazy day for his girls, even when his job was highly stressful.

I stole the idea of Daddy Dates from our neighbors who had two girls who were four and seven years older than Danielle. One Sunday late afternoon when I was playing with the girls out front, I saw our neighbor, Toni, reading on her patio. We struck up a conversation, and I commented on how relaxing it looked. She explained that George, her husband, had taken the girls to a movie. It was their arrangement that he took them on regular "daddy dates" to have special time with them. He usually only took one at a time, but they both had wanted to go this time. That was just the idea I needed to help Dan have some individual time with each girl, so this is when we started Daddy Date Night.

The first week, Dan took Danielle out on a date. She got to pick the place (*surprise! She chose McDonald's, which was a real treat for her*), and could even get a Happy Meal with a toy. We never bought three Happy Meals because we would split their food among themselves and we couldn't split a toy. We would order one hamburger, a six-piece chicken nuggets, one order of large fries, and three milks. Each child ate a third of a hamburger, two chicken nuggets, some fries, and drank their own milk. We were lucky we never started the Happy Meal habit, as many of our friends who had yielded to the Happy Meal habit would wind up yelling at the kids to eat their food when they just wanted to get into the play land.

On Danielle's date with her dad, I stayed home with Ashley and Lindsey. We watched a movie to make it special, too. The next week would be Ashley's turn to have a date with Daddy. And finally the third week would be Lindsey's turn. We decided to keep it simple. The last week of the month would be a family date night. I was glad we left the last week as a family date night, because if someone was sick or schedules got messed up, we could easily stay on schedule and just skip the family date night.

The girls loved having date nights with Daddy, but Dan got tired of going out every week. Sometimes he wanted to stay at home with the girls, which worked out well since I was feeling antsy with always being at home since I was already at home with the girls all day anyway.

From that, we started Mommy Date Nights. The next month it was my turn to take a girl out each week while Dan stayed home. Again, we ended the month with a family date night, and we alternated which months were Daddy Date Night months, and which were Mommy's. The girls loved date nights, and even as parents, we enjoyed having one-on-one time with each of the girls. It was amazing what I could learn about my child when I focused on one of them alone.

And even though I felt competent and excited to have all of these wonderful offensive ideas and plans, I had a terrible time keeping track. That led to arguments, which was exactly what Special Day and Date Nights were supposed to end. One night as I finished reading Ashley's book (because it was her special day), I heard Lindsey say it was her turn next.

"No, it's Danielle's turn, then your turn," I said, as I

grew frustrated.

That's when Ashley pointed out: "Daddy always goes Danielle, Ashley, and Lindsey."

"He does?" I questioned. And they all nodded in agreement.

So when I got done reading their books and the girls were tucked in for the night, I asked Dan about it. He pointed out that of course he went in age order. I was shocked! I went in alphabetical order. Well, *of course* that was what was causing all of the arguments! We needed a system. I told Dan that I would create a system, but he had to start going in alphabetical order. He agreed.

> *Develop a system with your spouse to prevent miscommunication.*

My system was specially designed to help keep track of: Special Day, Date Nights, and which parent was reading the books at night. I had been writing the date nights on the calendar, but there were times things had to change because Dan would end up working late or someone would be sick, so my calendar was often confusing.

To make it so *everyone* could see it, I developed a chart on poster board with: 'Special Day', 'Read Books' and 'Date Night' written on it.

I then grabbed eight clothespins. I made two for each girl, and labeled them with the first letter of their

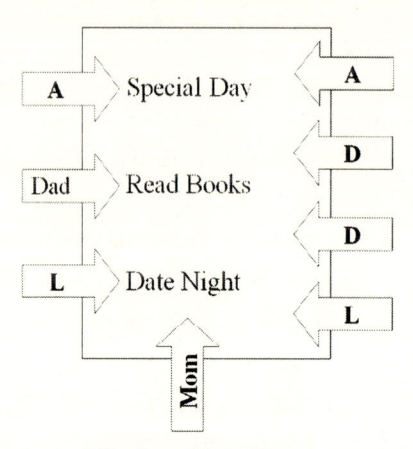

Clothes Pin Chart

names (two D, two A, and two L). I made two more that each had a Dad side and a Mom side also. (See the example poster.) I put 'A' clothespin for Ashley's turn for her Special Day. I turned the parent clothespin to Dad for his turn to read books. For Date Night, I put the L clothespin and the Mom side of the clothespin to show it was Mommy's turn to take Lindsey on a date. The extras went on the right side of the chart.

The poster was in balance with clothespins on each side. I put the poster up near the kitchen table so that each morning at breakfast, we moved the girls' clothespins in alphabetical order. The parent clothespin just got turned over to the other side. If, for some reason, the person who was supposed to do bedtime wasn't able to do it, then their name simply stayed there for the next night. Having this poster worked very well. If there was any question about whose turn it was, we would go to the poster and read it. When Lindsey would be mad that it wasn't her turn, we would blame the poster. She would be mad, but not at me for saying it wasn't her turn. It was the *poster's* fault. If there was any whining on who went second, we always defaulted the next girl *alphabetically*. And now Dan and I were on the same page on that, too.

Recovery: Needing Time to Recharge

In any game, there needs to be recovery time *between* games. In the game of parenthood, to be the best parents we could be meant we would have to find time to refuel ourselves and to take care of our relationship, and this started happening when we were able to be on the offense. The ability to have a smooth bedtime routine kept the house peaceful, and when I would come downstairs after tucking the girls in, Dan would have the supper dishes done and the toys all put away (or vice versa), and both of us could sit and relax together. It was a great time to talk and reconnect. Dan could share his workday, especially the issues he didn't want to talk about in front of the girls, and I could tell him about the girls' day without having *them* relive it, and we could share about how much (and how rapidly!) they were changing. Being able to talk without little ears around—even simple adult conversation about updating our schedules or planning future events—was something we grew to deeply appreciate. Many nights we were too tired to have much conversation, but it was nice just to be alone together and recharge our relationship's batteries.

Early on, we both knew how important it was to have time away from the kids . . . to go out on a *real* date by ourselves. My mom was the first one who pushed us out the door that first time we left infant Danielle. She was also there when I was in the hospital delivering our next child, and she always insisted Dan and I make time to go out alone as we adjusted to having an additional child. She knew how important refueling was to our marriage.

Each time we did it, it was hard to leave the girls behind, even for a few hours. This continued as the girls grew, but each time my mom visited us, she insisted and we were grateful . . . but sometimes those visits were not often enough.

One year, Dan had a work Christmas party coming up that I knew we should attend and my Mom was not going to be able to help us out, so it was time for us to hire a babysitter. I asked other parents for recommendations, and I found a babysitter named Kelly who was right in our neighborhood.

The first time we hired Kelly, I was seven months pregnant with Lindsey. Dan and I went out for dinner and were gone just a couple of hours. Remember this was before cell phones, so I couldn't call or text easily to check-in with her. When Dan and I got home, both girls were sound asleep in their beds and the toys were picked up. We were able to go to our Christmas party with me only making two calls from a pay phone to check in with Kelly.

We were able to have Kelly babysit for us a few more times. It was so nice to have time as a couple, and I was adjusting to having a teenager take care of our two girls. One morning after Kelly had babysat, I was getting Ashley and Danielle ready for the day. I set Ashley on the bed and as I was putting on her shoes, and she said, "Mommy, can I jump on the bed?"

"No, we don't jump on the bed," I answered, wondering why she didn't remember that rule.

"Kelly lets us," Ashley explained.

So the babysitter let's you jump on the bed? I thought to myself. Out loud, I asked, "Is Kelly sitting right here when you are jumping on the bed?" Ashley nodded, so I went on to explain: "Sometimes babysitters have different rules than Mommy and Daddy. But you should always ask me if the babysitter's rule is okay."

"Okay," she replied and started to jump on the bed. I reminded her that while Mommy is here, we didn't jump on the bed. As I walked out of the room, I felt a sense of peace come over me. I realized that I would hear from Ashley if things were different when there was a babysitter in the house, letting me relax even more when a babysitter was taking care of the girls.

We continued leaving Danielle and Ashley with a babysitter after Lindsey was born, as Dan and I were asked to lead an infant class for community education since we were experienced parents. Parents were welcome to bring their babies, so we brought Lindsey. We just had to get a babysitter for the other two, and we were only gone two hours total, so a couple of times we hired a new babysitter, Jessica. Dan and I actually enjoyed having just a couple of hours together out of the house each week. We even liked having just one child with us for a special time. When we returned home, the girls were in their pajamas, in their beds, and sound asleep. Everything seemed to be fine. It wasn't until the next week when Danielle and Ashley were excited to see the babysitter that I felt confident in leaving them with her again, even for two hours.

Things were going so well with the babysitter that Dan and I thought we would try to leave all three girls with her. Kelly was busy, so we asked Jessica, who had only babysat the two girls a couple of times. Being nervous and worried that adding a baby to the mix might be more of a challenge than a teenager could handle, I hit the record button on the phone message machine before we left. We would be able to hear everything that happened in the kitchen until the tape ran out. (Perhaps not ethical, but I just had to know.) When I listened to the recording I heard Jessica talking very nicely to Danielle and Ashley. I heard her playing with them and then started a movie for them to watch. Then I heard her talking on the phone to a friend as the tape ran out. All sounded great until I realized I never heard Lindsey or her caring for Lindsey.

So I re-listened to the tape, and that's when I heard it.

There was music playing in the background. I figured she had wound up one of Lindsey's musical toys to keep her content. It wasn't until the next day when I turned on Lindsey's mobile over her crib when I laid her down for her nap. It was the music from her mobile. The babysitter had laid Lindsey in her crib after we left! I was so sad that she stuck Lindsey upstairs in her bed while she was downstairs. I held Lindsey extra all day. When I told Dan about it that night, he pointed out that Lindsey was not crying and it was only one night— but we never hired Jessica again.

> *Others will care for your children differently, but you determine if their method is acceptable.*

It took awhile for us to hire another babysitter. It was a combination of what had happened the first time we left all three girls and us just being so busy. Once again, Dan's work Christmas party was coming up, so it was time. This time we decided to hire two babysitters so they could work together with the girls and get them all to bed. I talked with Kelly, who we trusted, to see if she had a friend she could invite over to help her with the girls. I explained that this was still a job and our girls came first.

Of course I was worried that the babysitting friends would be tempted to just hang out with each other and ignore the kids. So we went out a couple of times before the big Christmas party to try it out. One night we told them we were going out to eat, a movie, and would stop for drinks afterwards so wouldn't be home until 11:00 p.m. but after just one drink, we were so sleepy that we were headed home by ten. The two teenagers sat on the couch, watching a movie and eating popcorn. The girls were all in bed, sound asleep, and the house was all picked up. I was comforted by what I saw. But to be sure all went well, I asked Ashley about it the next day. She said they had a blast and told me every game they played together. We had found two responsible babysitters! Now we were ready to go to the Christmas party, stay late, and know our girls were well-cared for and would have fun.

◆ ◆ ◆

True refueling came when we would take a long weekend away from our girls. We were very lucky that my mom loved to take care of them and was very happy to arrange her schedule to watch them for us. I always made a huge list of their schedule and anything I could think of that she may need to know. Without hesitation, she would always say to me, "You know I just do whatever I want, right?"

I explained to her that I wasn't sure that was real comforting, but I knew the list was there for her to use if she needed it. I trusted my mom and knew that the girls were safe and loved.

Both Dan and I spent most of the weekend thinking of the girls and talking about them, but it was still nice to have quality couple time. When we returned, the girls were very excited to see us and had many stories to tell about what Grandma did with them. I even learned that Grandma didn't make toast the same way I did. She cut it into triangles and I just cut it in half, horizontally. I realized the girls were building a stronger relationship with their grandma and appreciating their mom a little bit more, too.

One Memorial Day weekend, we decided to go away for our tenth anniversary. The girls were five, six, and seven years old. I had the list for Grandma, reviewed it with her, and ignored her comment that she wouldn't use it. Dan had everything loaded in the car, and just as I bent down to kiss Danielle goodbye, I realized she had a fever. I said, "Mom, the baby medicine is in the bathroom medicine cabinet; she will need some. Good luck."

Grandma Gin is Lindsey's Show and Tell

I didn't think twice as we walked out the door, as Mom reassured me they would be fine. As the weekend continued, I didn't worry any more than usual. When we called to check in, we found out that Ashley came down with a fever the next day, too, and two girls were sick. They were doing fine, but were doing more relaxing activities than usual. I knew that I should enjoy my weekend, because on Tuesday morning we would be in the doctor's office getting them checked out and I would need lots of patience for the sick and crabby kids. That is when we realized we had matured as parents. We were able to let my mom take care of our girls, even when they were sick. We knew they were loved by Grandma while we were gone. We returned as better parents for taking time to refuel ourselves, and our marriage was stronger for taking time for our relationship. Refueling was an important part of our offense!

In the Rearview Mirror of The Parent Offense

Looking back, I understand that not everyone has the same concerns as parents. Some like to have their kids stay up late and are more go-with-the-flow type of parents. A specific bedtime was very valuable—and worked—for us, but I understand every family is different. As I reflect, I realize that the personality of the girls affected our routines and made me keep them more structured, even if I personally am not. I learned that it was easier for me as the adult to change than to force the girls to change.

The girls needed both of us, but I always had to remind myself that they needed their daddy. A daddy who constantly juggled his work schedule so he could be there for his girls. A daddy who taught each of them how to ride a bicycle, even putting the training wheels back on when the process of learning was too scary. A daddy that spent hours playing sports with his girls, building their confidence as they learned. Dan has always been a devoted father who chose his family over career advancement many times.

Recovery time was so very significant for us to do almost every day. When the stress level in our lives started rising, it was also when we filled our recovery time with other tasks. We found ourselves overwhelmed and short tempered. That would lead to disagreements, which forced us to stop and talk. It was then that we would realize we needed time to recover. We would once again take time each day, but it was a constant lesson we repeated. Not only did I need time for myself to recover each day, but Dan and I needed time as a couple– if not daily, then hopefully weekly. Most of the time it was after the girls were in bed, but it was crucial to have date nights. I had to learn to put the needs of our marriage first as long as the girls were safely cared for by a responsible person.

As I look back at hiring my first babysitter, it felt strange that I wanted to talk to the mom of our babysitter, but it just felt like the right thing to do. Then when my girls were old enough to babysit, I talked to the parent who was hiring them. I needed to know my teenage girls were safe, too. Dan always had me drive or walk the female babysitter home. He didn't want them to feel uncomfortable and he didn't want them to make up some story of him being inappropriate. Not a bad idea.

There were so many times when life's demands caused a distance between the two of us. We didn't have a disagreement. We were just busy and silently growing apart. By having at least a weekend away as a couple each year helped eliminate that distance. It was vital to give our marriage the gift of time without the girls.

Section II:
MOM AS A CAREER

Chapter 4:
Feeling Like an Intern

I thought I understood what being a mom was all about. When I was a Home Economics teacher, I taught a Parenting class. I actually said, "I don't need to be a parent to understand parenting. A history teacher doesn't have to live history to teach history." I apologize to my students. I was wrong! I didn't have a clue what parenting was all about!

Orientation Day: Bonding Time

As a new mom, I was glad for the instructions that the hospital provided. I was taught how to change and breastfeed Danielle. The very first message on feeding my baby was that my breast was no longer a private part. The nurse touched and adjusted my breast and Danielle as needed. She told me to just relax, and walked out of the room as if I knew what I was doing. *Sure*, I thought, *relax*? I discovered I was humming to myself to relax. (That was a behavior I started when I was a child growing up; whenever I was scared I would sing. When I would have to go out to the barn at night or down in the old basement, I would sing to myself to relax.) Now without even thinking about it, I was humming to my baby. I started to relax. I felt my shoulders drop about four inches. The nurse didn't leave me because I knew what I was doing; she left me to give me some privacy. I may have panicked . . . just a little.

Of course I had read about breastfeeding before I had Danielle. However, I had not read about how breastfeeding hurts, or did I skip over that paragraph? The nurse returned in a few minutes to see how things were going and I asked her about the pain.

The nurse said, "You have to let your breast get tough."

I wondered, *How will my breast get tough? Did I really want tough breasts? What about this cramping . . . was I having my period already?*

But the nurse clarified that in time, it doesn't hurt as much.

"You might start to feel your uterus contracting to get back to its smaller size. Breast feeding helps that," she also explained.

So now I was humming to the baby to keep myself from screaming in pain. I started wondering if this breastfeeding thing was worth it. I was sure I would be fine if I my uterus got back to its normal size on its own without breastfeeding helping it contract. I now completely understood why many women chose not to breastfeed. I continued to tough it out and kept humming. I learned about different positions to hold my baby when breastfeeding to help with attachment and my pain. I was instructed to always alternate which side I started on with each feeding, as the baby sucks the strongest in the beginning. I was even given a hint to put a safety pin on my nursing bra for where to start next time. It took me a week to figure out what song I was humming to myself every time I was breastfeeding. It was the folksong "Kumbaya" so that became Danielle's special song. Decidedly not a cute baby song, but I didn't know I was going to need to sing. I had never listened to children's music before becoming a mom, so it was the best I could do.

In nothing flat, I had to re-learn the breastfeeding thing again with Ashley. At first I started humming, "Kumbaya," but then I realized Ashley should have her own song. So I started singing "Rock-a-bye Baby." I realized when I got to the end and the baby falls, that perhaps it wasn't the best song to sing, but for the life of me, I couldn't think of any other songs, but "Kumbaya", or "Rock-a-bye Baby," so I just sang, "Rock-a-bye Baby" lovingly all the way through to the end. I was glad I was singing because breastfeeding hurt more this time. I thought maybe I just didn't remember the intensity of the pain, but when the nurse came in to check on me, she said, "You may have more pain with contractions this time. Your body seems to react more with second pregnancies. If you have a third it will be even more intense."

Once again, I had not read in my books that the pain could be worse, and no one told me!

> *Everyone shares their birth stories, but physical adjustments afterwards are often kept a secret.*

I once again was singing through the pain to help me relax and not focus on the changes my body was going through. Music and singing helped me relax and change my focus from my pain to my baby as I looked down on my new little Ashley and thought about how special this moment was for us. The music gave me the calm I needed to enjoy the moment.

The third time around with nursing was not a charm, but at least this time I was prepared. The earlier nurse had prepared me with the information that the pain could even be worse this time and she was right; with Lindsey, it *was* more intense . . . but I was ready for it. It helped me to know that it was going to hurt more. I also had planned ahead this time and memorized a song for Lindsey. I changed the words of the lullaby "Hush Little Baby, Don't Say a Word" to Mama instead of Papa. Since there were so many different verses for me to focus on, it really helped to keep my mind off the pain. By my third baby, I felt like a veteran breastfeeding mom, which made things a lot easier. I was actually able to relax.

That feeling made the temporary pain of adjusting to the breastfeeding process worth it. When I would attach my newborn to my breast, I would look down at her as she sucked for nourishment. I was in love. I was holding her next to my heart and feeling her skin next to my skin. My body was physically giving her a part of me to help her survive. At the same time, my heart was already willing to give her everything to make her happy. The intensity of the combined emotional and physical feelings (coupled with bouts of exhaustion) together sometimes caused tears to run down my face. But those feelings of joy were rekindled each time I would feed my daughter.

✧ ✧ ✧

As emotionally satisfying as breastfeeding was, it was totally demoralizing to not be successful at it. When Danielle was only three months old, she became a very fussy baby. I struggled to find any solution. One day, Dan and I met at a restaurant for lunch and he suggested that she was still hungry. I told him I had just fed her she couldn't be hungry, but he insisted that she acted hungry. When I got home, I called the pediatric nurse and asked her for suggestions. Of course she agreed with Dan. She suggested after I feed her the next time, I try to offer her a bottle. If she drank more than two ounces, I was not producing enough milk for her and that I should start supplementing with formula. That first bottle, Danielle drank six ounces.

As I held her and she drank and drank, I cried and cried. I was starving my baby. I was a failure. I didn't even know she was hungry. What a terrible mother I was! (Why do I always beat myself up?) After a pity party, a talk with a lactation specialist, and support from Dan that night, I was finally able to accept that the stress of moving and being a new mom had taken its toll. I was not a failure; my body just needed a little help. So

I would breastfeed her first thing in the morning. The next time she was hungry I would give her a bottle. I would switch between breastfeeding and a bottle every other feeding. I was warned that she might not continue to breastfeed, that she may prefer a bottle, but she did both. Thank goodness! I don't think I was ready emotionally for that type of rejection.

Ashley had refused a bottle from the time she was three months old. I was stuck breastfeeding her for *every* feeding. Whenever I was away from her, I had to plan to be back in time to feed her. As she got older, I struggled with my lack of freedom. I started to feed her formula from a sippy cup. She accepted that much easier than a bottle. She started drinking from a sippy cup at six months whenever I was not there to breastfeed her. By the time she was finished breastfeeding, I was relieved.

When I was breastfeeding Lindsey, I enjoyed every minute, knowing this was going to be my last time. Thankfully, she was cooperative with her weaning. After she was seven months old, I was able to taper off the breastfeeding. I was breastfeeding her at bedtime and nap time, and then it was getting stressful at bedtime with getting all of the girls into bed, so I stopped breastfeeding at night. When she was nine months old, I was only breastfeeding her before her afternoon nap. (I was just not ready to be done.) One day, I was so busy with all the girls that I just put her down for a nap without thinking. It wasn't until she was sound asleep that I realized I had forgotten to breastfeed her. I guess *she* didn't need it, I did. But that day through my busyness, I was done, too. I was sad, but I was ready.

Where are the Instructions?

Even though I didn't get a degree to become a mom, I thought I was ready for the job. However, the first time Danielle was crying and didn't need to eat, had just been changed, and had already burped, I wished I knew more. Many times Dan and I would joke, "Why don't babies come with an instruction manual?"

When we had Danielle, the hospital offered instruction. Dan and I learned how to change diapers and how to give Danielle both a sponge bath and a real bath while still supporting her head. We had to attend a class and learn about infant car seats before I was discharged. (When the other girls were born there were no classes offered. The hospital stay was a day shorter, too.)

Without an instruction manual, I just had to trust myself. I found myself trusting my gut as I had done before in my in life. Within the first few hours of Danielle's birth, I watched her find her thumb, just like she had in the ultrasound. But later when they brought her back to me, she had sleeves that covered her hands, and when I asked, they explained it was so she wouldn't cut herself with her nails. I didn't like that reasoning and I would fold down the sleeves every time they brought her to me. I didn't want her to not to be able to find the comfort of her thumb. I was developing my mommy instincts.

By the time I left the hospital with Danielle, I had all of

the information, but absolutely felt like a rookie. That was proven to me when I went to change her the first time. Even though I had a lesson on how to put on a diaper, it was a disposable in the hospital. We had decided to use cloth diapers and using pins next to my tiny baby was tricky. (Back then it was to save money, not to preserve the environment.) I quickly learned it was difficult to get the cloth diaper tight so it didn't leak. After she peed through both her clothes and mine, I got better.

Danielle was only home a few days when she cut her face with her fingernails. I felt so bad, but I still didn't want to cover her hands, so I had to figure out how to cut her fingernails. Actually, it wasn't a matter of figuring it out . . . it was finding the guts. Taking a sharp object next to her tiny hands was very scary. The first time, *I* jumped with each clip, but she didn't move. The next time I cut her nails while she was sleeping. If it did wake her, it was only for a moment, but she held still and it was much easier than clipping a moving target.

✧ ✧ ✧

What surprised me were the intense emotions of being a mom. I distinctly remember laying a screaming three-month-old Danielle down in her crib. I knew I had just changed and fed her, but she continued to scream as I walked down the steps. I realized I had never felt such intense frustration. I had no idea what to do to console her; I didn't know what she wanted. This tiny little thing was driving me crazy! I am sure the lack of sleep was adding to my emotional state. After a few moments of deep breathing and a few tears, I walked back up the steps and picked her up. She stopped crying and laid her head on my shoulder. As I descended the steps I felt such intense love. How could such a tiny baby make me feel so incapable yet so loved? Then I realized all she wanted was a calm, relaxed mommy.

Being a new mom was an adjustment, even when I had my second child. Ashley was just one week old and my mom was leaving when I had a panic attack at the idea. She had arrived the day Ashley was born and helped me adjust to having a newborn and a 15-month-old . . . and now she was leaving.

How would I cope? What would I do if both kids needed me at the same time?

Both Dan and Mom tried to reassure me, but I was a mess. Finally, she agreed to come back in just five days; two days were the weekend, so I decided I could make it three days if she promised she would be back. The adjustment to mothering a newborn and a toddler was more than I could deal with on my own. When Mom returned, she helped me gain confidence that I could handle it on my own. She helped me with household tasks more than she helped with the girls. I was able to learn that while I was breastfeeding, I could watch Danielle play in the same room. She didn't have to be entertained. When one girl needed changing, I would check the other one to see if *she* needed changing. Most important, Mom reminded me to sleep while Ashley napped. The cleaning and picking up she could do or when she wasn't there, Dan could do it at night. By the end of her second visit, I was emotionally ready to handle two children.

> *It's a gift to have family or friends to help you adjust to motherhood.*

I didn't realize it at the time, but when Lindsey was born I had lots of support. My family made sure I wasn't left on my own too soon or too long. My mom ended up staying with us for almost three weeks, with that first week devoted to helping me with the two toddlers, as I was painfully overdue. After Lindsey was born, Mom helped entertain the older kids as I gained my strength back. But soon she focused on household tasks so I would gain confidence in dealing with three children. After my mom left, my sister came for a week when Dan had to leave town on business. I needed to have another adult around for emotional support. Slowly, I learned that I could only do so much at one time, and the girls had to adjust to waiting their turn.

In short order, I did gain confidence that I could handle all three of them on my own. It was just normal to have three girls, each just over a year apart. Sometimes I had too much confidence, or I just didn't think things through before I did them.

An example of this was when Ashley was about to celebrate her third birthday and Dan was out of town and going to miss it. I wanted to make it special for Ashley without stressing out by trying to do it all myself, so I decided we would celebrate with the extended family . . . who all lived four hours away. My mom was willing to host the party, and we invited my siblings, along with Dan's parents and brothers. I was excited instead of dreading her birthday, so I packed myself and the girls up and we left the house just before afternoon naps were to start. I had driven for about one hour when Lindsey woke up and started to cry. Both Danielle and Ashley were asleep and would nap for another hour, but not if Lindsey woke them up. And if I stopped to comfort Lindsey, Ashley would certainly wake up the minute I stopped. It was then I realized how stupid this idea really was. I was driving four hours by myself with a 19-month-old, a three-year-old, and a four-year-old. What in the world was I thinking? I started to panic.

So I did what I always do when I'm anxious or nervous: I started singing. At first, I sang whatever came to mind. She was now crying softly. Then I remembered and started singing her lullaby, "Hush Little Baby," and she stopped crying and looked around. I continued to sing and she just listened. I sang for a really long time, and each time I stopped she started to whimper. Finally, she was asleep. I shook my head and reminded myself that I truly was a crazy mom.

> *There are times when things are just overwhelming. Find your way to stay calm.*

Group Projects: Sharing or Taking Turns

One morning as I was busy paying bills at the table, two-year-old Danielle and baby Ashley—who was learning to crawl– were playing in the room. Suddenly I heard Ashley cry, so I got up to give her the toy I thought Danielle had taken from her. As I sat back down, I realized that Ashley had been on the other side of the room just a minute ago, so now my curiosity was piqued as to what *really* happened. So I watched, and within a few minutes, Ashley crawled across the room to where Danielle was playing, sat up, and let out a cry. I went over and moved Ashley back to where she had come from, and she continued to cry. I realized that for weeks, I had been disciplining Danielle for taking a toy from her sister, when all along, Ashley had learned that all she had to do was crawl over to her sister, cry, and then she would get Danielle's toy.

This had started months before when I would put Ashley on a blanket on the floor. I taught Danielle that the toys on the blanket were Ashley's toys, and that she wasn't to play on Ashley's blanket or take the toys I had put there for Ashley. However, I had not kept up with the changes that were happening. Ashley was now able to move off the blanket and go to *Danielle's* toys. I had assumed that Danielle was still taking Ashley's toys away, but it turned out that it was the other way around! Well, not any more. I had finally figured out her game!

> *Take time to observe your child;*
> *you will learn a great deal.*

As I continued to watch their interactions, I saw that

sometimes Danielle would quietly share her toy. Just as Ashley would make it to where Danielle was playing, she would set her toy down and pick up another one and let Ashley play alongside of her. Other times, Danielle didn't want to share and she would turn her back on Ashley to try to keep her away. That was when Ashley would cry because she didn't get that toy. So I would walk over to them and ask Danielle if she wanted to share with Ashley.

"No," she said.

So as I moved Ashley, I said, "You will get your turn next."

When Danielle would walk away from the toy, I'd ask her, "Can you give that toy to Ashley? It's her turn now." She was happy to do it because she was able to finish with it first. It didn't take long for Danielle to learn to speak for herself and say, 'No' when Ashley would get too close to her toys. Then she learned to tell her, 'Next' when she was done as she handed Ashley the toy.

It wasn't long before the tides turned. Ashley was more mobile and vocal and would be playing with a toy, and Danielle would come up and start playing with it. In these moments, Ashley would cry, "Mine."

I told Danielle she would have to play with something else until Ashley was done, but that was the start of them fighting over everything. I started to comprehend that sibling rivalry didn't really start until the baby was mobile.

One afternoon when I was holding one-year-old Ashley on my lap, and we were enjoying a little cuddling time, it wasn't long before two-year-old Danielle wanted to join in, so I reached down and scooped her up. My lap was big enough for both girls, but they didn't act like it. Danielle began pushing Ashley, and then Ashley kicked back. In no time at all, a nice hug turned ugly, *fast*. I put both girls down and said, "Enough!" I was at the end of my rope.

I was frustrated that we couldn't just have a little cuddle time without them fighting over me. I thought they should be able to share me like they did their toys. As that thought went through my head, I realized they didn't share their toys like that. They were taking turns, yet, I wanted my girls to share *me*, at the same time, no matter what. If they couldn't share Mommy, then Mommy was done hugging everyone.

With this new thought in mind, I sat back down on the couch and waited. It wasn't long before Danielle climbed onto my lab. She even glared at her sister with an 'I got Mommy' look. So Ashley quickly responded with her arms stretched up for me to pick her up. I turned to Danielle and asked her, "Can Ashley sit here, too?"

"No!" was her quick response.

I looked down at Ashley and explained, "It's Danielle's turn for Mommy Time. When she is done it will be your turn."

She sat on my feet and cried. I handed her blanket to her and she waited, sadly. Within minutes, Danielle climbed down and said, "Hiya's turn."

I scooped up Ashley and we cuddled for a few

minutes. Then, off she went to play. Cuddle time ended without me frustrated. I still wasn't sure if I had found *the* solution to the problem, but it had worked once so I was going to keep trying it.

The next day, Danielle sat on my lap while we watched TV, and Ashley came over to join us. I turned to Danielle and asked, "Would you like to share Mommy or take turns?"

Danielle was confused with my question. I explained she was getting Mommy Time first. So she could decide if she wanted to share Mommy with Ashley or have Mommy Time all by herself.

"Share," she said. Shocked, I scooped Ashley up and sat her on the other side of my lap. Ashley smiled and cuddled. As I waited, no one pushed or kicked. They both just sat on my lap, content.

This was the start of Mommy Time. Whenever I was holding one girl and another would want in, the first one there was given the option to decide if we shared or took turns. Sometimes the answer was to take turns, so I would cuddle with just them. It amazed me that it never took long for them to climb down and say to the other, "Your turn."

Other times, both girls would sit happily on my lap with no bickering, kicking, or pushing. They realized, at that young age, that *they* were making the decision and the decision was not being forced onto them. I knew I had discovered the answer when Danielle climbed onto my lap and yelled, "Hiya, come, it's Mommy Time."

I was so lucky we had established this before

Lindsey was born. When Lindsey was breastfeeding and Ashley would try to climb on my lap, I would pretend to ask infant Lindsey if she wanted to let Ashley join in. I was able to decide what I *heard* Lindsey say: "It's my turn; your turn next."

I could finish feeding Lindsey in peace. Once I put Lindsey down for her nap, I would give Ashley her turn. It was nice to have Mommy Time for each girl separately.

Sometimes I would *hear* Lindsey say, "Yes, if you sit next to Mommy, you can join us." I would pull Ashley next to me on the couch and we would watch TV together while I breastfed Lindsey. Not to be left out, Danielle would soon be climbing up on the couch, trying to sit *between* Ashley and me. So first I asked Lindsey if it was okay for Danielle to join us. If I *heard* her say, 'yes', then I would turn to Ashley to ask if she wanted Danielle to join us. She was there next, so she had a chance to decide, too. Most of the time, she didn't mind since she was just sitting next to me anyway. Now we all had to move over so I was in the middle of the couch to leave room on both sides. That was why it was so nice to have baby Lindsey decide if we were going to share. If I was almost done feeding her, the answer would be for each girl wait her turn. This would save me moving everyone over for just a few more minutes.

It didn't take long for the girls to figure out my game with Lindsey talking and they would say, "Lindsey said it was okay for me to join the Mommy Time." I thought it was so cute; I let them decide for Lindsey.

There were times when I would take so long with

baby Lindsey that the girl waiting for Mommy Time had found other things to do. I would still ask them if they wanted Mommy Time, and when they said no, I felt badly. Then I realized the real reason they wanted to sit by me was because they were feeling left out when my attention was on one of the other girls. They didn't care anymore because I wasn't dividing my attention any longer.

Of course, being a busy mom of three little girls, sometimes I would totally forget. By the time I put baby Lindsey down, I couldn't remember who wanted to sit by me, or if anyone cared. To remedy this, after laying Lindsey down for her nap, I got into the habit of asking if anyone wanted Mommy Time.

When baby Lindsey would cry and one of the girls was already on my lap for Mommy Time, I was reminded – many times – as they would invariably say, "My turn."

All I had to remember to do was ask them if they would share Mommy Time with Lindsey. Even if they said no, with a crying infant in the background, it wasn't long before they'd climb down and say, "Lindsey's turn."

✧ ✧ ✧

When Danielle would play with other children, she didn't seem to care if they took her toys. She would just walk away and find something else to play with. I started to worry that I had taught her to share *too well*. I thought she needed to fight back and keep that toy and I was worried she would grow up with other people taking advantage of her. I remember thinking, *Why would you teach a child to fight back?* And at the same time, I wondered, *How would you even begin to do that?* I remember saying to other children that Danielle had this or that, but Danielle would just turn and walk away, making me look silly. Luckily, on her second birthday, she received a toy car, and absolutely loved it. She just sat inside of it even though the other kids at the birthday party wanted a turn in her car. They would pull open the door and she wouldn't let them in. She was fighting back!

One parent even told Danielle that she had to share and started to pull her out of the car, but I stopped that parent. I explained this was her very first time in her new car, and that she was not done yet. I had a lot of strange looks from parents who didn't think I was a good mom because I wasn't teaching my daughter to share. But in that moment, I was a very proud mom. I already knew she could share, but now I was able to witness her fighting for something that was important to her.

Danielle won't share

As Danielle got older, I started to realize that she was walking away from the toys because she was moving on to the next toy. She actually didn't want to share with someone else; she liked to play by herself. She would rather move on to another toy than have to play with

THAT toy with someone else. That didn't upset her because she was content to find the next thing. It wasn't that she wouldn't fight for what she wanted; it was that she was done. She was more interested in seeing what else she could play with, which worked out well for Ashley, who would just follow her around and play with whatever she left behind.

By contrast, Ashley would cry the minute another child got into her personal space around the toys she was playing with. She didn't even wait for them to touch her toy! I tried to work with her to share, but she didn't like to do it. She didn't want anyone playing *with* her, or many times, even *near* her. I hadn't realized that I had said take turns at home all of the time, but when I was with other moms and children, we all said, 'share'. Ashley didn't like to share, but she *would* take turns. So, instead of saying 'share' to Ashley, I started saying 'take turns,' and she understood the difference.

> *Listen to the words you are using; do you really mean what you are saying?*

Lindsey loved to share. She was the one going up to take the toys away from others. She wanted to play with or alongside them. She didn't like to play by herself and wanted to be in the middle of the fun. With Lindsey, I had to remind her often, "Who had it first?'

But she would say, "Me too." She actually didn't want to take the toy away; she wanted to play *with* them. But that was not how other children viewed her actions.

Believe me; I didn't figure this out when they were always fighting with their toys. I had no idea they were trying to accomplish different things with their toys. I was only focused on who had it first, because that child got to decide if they wanted to share it or take turns. But if I didn't know who had it first, my solution was to *put the toy in time-out*. I couldn't put the child in time-out for fighting over the toy because I didn't know who was wrong. So the toy went in time-out on top of the kitchen cabinets, which only I could reach.

I usually took the toy down when the girls were off to the next thing, but sometimes it would stay up there for a few days (because I forgot about it). Sometimes one of the girls would happen to think of it and ask if that toy was still in time-out.

One day, I was reminding the girls that a few of their friends were coming over to play. Ashley asked if she could put a toy in time-out. At first I didn't understand, so she explained that she didn't like to share her certain toy because her friend, Nathan, didn't play with it right. I realized that was an excellent idea, as long as it was just a few special toys. We decided to put them in my bedroom, which was off limits for the other kids to go in, before they arrived.

Trust Yourself

My confidence as Mom came from the advice of one special doctor who I saw only twice. When Danielle was only six weeks old, I took her to her well-baby check-up with a pediatrician and we were moving to Rochester the very next day. First, he confirmed she was a healthy, growing, and happy baby. The doctor answered all of my concerns and then I asked for any advice he could give me since I was moving away. He said, "Trust yourself. You are the mom, and you know your child best."

I looked at him so confused; I had only been a mom for six weeks. I wondered *how* I could know best.

"Many times, doctors try to tell mothers their child is fine," he said. "Because what we see at that moment fits within the normal range. But if you know this is *not* normal for your child, then say that. Fight for your child. Demand your child be seen and that you are heard. You are the mom and you know *your* child best," he went on to explain.

I walked out of that doctor's office scared to death. I didn't know what Danielle's cries meant. I was guessing most of the time. How did I know best? I had been a Mom for six weeks. Nevertheless, I would think of those words often as my experience as a mom grew. I *did* know best. I developed confidence to persuade the nurses when they tried to push me aside on the phone, sometimes making me feel like my concerns weren't justified or I was being an over protective mom.

After Ashley had her six-month immunizations, she just wasn't herself. She was being very clingy and was unusually lethargic. At first, I didn't think anything of it, but as the day wore on I became more worried. I called the doctor's office back and told the nurse about Ashley's behavior. Since there was a chance of a reaction to the shots she received, they had me bring her back in to the doctor's office. They didn't see a reaction from the shots, but were worried about her lethargy and thought it might be meningitis . . . so they were going to do a spinal tap. They explained exactly what they would be doing and that I could wait here. I explained I would be with her and help calm her. (I could hear my first pediatrician's advice, 'trust yourself.') The nurse said that was not allowed.

I said, "Then you will not be doing the test. If I can't be there, she isn't having it done."

I knew Ashley's reaction to being restrained would definitely be a freak-out, so I was going to be sure she knew at least one person in the room. (I had a spinal tap in my pre-mom life and I knew how important holding still was to the procedure.) I pushed to protect the comfort of my child. The doctor returned to say, "I understand you will be in the room with us. I just want to be sure you can handle the needle and won't be in our way."

I confirmed I would be fine. I helped hold one side of Ashley still while having her look at me. I didn't watch what was happening; I just kept calmly looking at Ashley. She did great and the test was done in a few minutes. It ended up she didn't have meningitis, but they were not sure what was wrong with her. She didn't have the normal reaction to the shots, but that could have caused it. In a few days she was completely back to her normal self.

Trust yourself. Push for answers from the medical staff.

My confidence as a mom was growing with each experience. Lindsey was just over two years old when she got the flu in the middle of the night and it continued through the next day. When she wouldn't eat anything at supper, we decided I should take her to Urgent Care. I walked her around the waiting room, pointing out the Easter eggs hanging from the ceiling. She would hardly move her head to look. She was very content to sit on my lap and lean her head on my shoulder. That was not normal behavior for any two-year-old, especially Lindsey.

When we finally got in to see the doctor, he explained how she had the flu and there wasn't much he could give her. He just told me to be sure she had enough fluids and watch her through the night. I interrupted to ask him, "She has not kept anything down since last night. So how is she going to get enough fluids?"

He got defensive. "Do you want me to put her in the hospital?"

All I was concerned about was that she didn't get any worse, which is what I tried to explain to him. So he decided we would just give her some apple juice and see what happened. I was so confused. *Did he think I didn't know if she was throwing up or not? Even if she was my first two-year-old, I think I could tell if she was keeping things down or not!* In any case, I let her drink her apple juice, even though apple juice normally gave Lindsey diarrhea. I knew she wouldn't keep it down, so it didn't matter. And sure enough, just as he returned to the examining room, she threw up.

And yet, the doctor still figured she would be fine. He wanted me to take her home and check on her during the night to see if she got any worse. I quickly questioned him.

"She normally sleeps twelve hours at night and so when I lay her down when she gets home, how will I know if she is getting worse?"

He still thought I was an idiot, as he explained that I should wake her up to see if she was lethargic. As he looked at my puzzled face, he said again, "Do you want me to put her in the hospital?"

"No . . . I don't know," I said, confused. Then I asked him, "How would I know the difference between being half asleep in the middle of the night and worse than she is now?"

It was like he finally looked at her and saw how she looked for the first time. She still had her head on my shoulder, resting lethargically. He squeezed her fingertip to see how fast the blood flow would return. He started to realize that perhaps he had missed something. He sent in a nurse to draw some blood, but she left without getting the blood for some reason. She urgently explained to me that the doctor would be right in.

When he returned, he explained that I should take her directly to the hospital. I started to interrupt that I didn't want her to go to the hospital, but he stopped me. He told me that the nurse was unable to find a vein because Lindsey was dehydrated. I needed to take her directly to the hospital, do not stop at home!

Everything had changed.

Once she was admitted into the hospital, the nurse tried to find a vein. Lindsey needed fluid through an IV. The nurses asked me to leave, but I insisted otherwise. "I will be fine and I am not going anywhere!"

They could tell from my tone and body language that I was not leaving Lindsey's side. As I stood by her head and watched them search for a vein, I was scared. I started to sing, *"Hush little Baby, Don't Say a Word"* Lindsey's lullaby without even realizing it. I had tears running down my cheeks, but Lindsey was laying very still looking up at me, so I just kept singing. Before long, the nurses were done. Lindsey looked up at them and said, "Thank you."

With her cute little *thank you*, I was on the verge of bawling, but I dried my tears with my sleeve and just held my little girl. Later that night, one of the nurses was adjusting the IV and shared with me how awesome it was to have me in the room with Lindsey to keep her calm while they looked for a vein. She explained, "Most of the times parents get in the way, but you knew what was best for your child and you knew you could handle it. Then when Lindsey in her sweet little voice said 'thank you,' there wasn't a dry eye in the room. That's why I don't normally work Pediatrics."

I sat with Lindsey in the hospital for five days as she recovered from the flu. One of the first days she was napping, I forced myself to leave her side. As I headed down the elevator to the cafeteria, I tried to decide if I should just grab some food and head back or if I should take a break for a few minutes. I heard my mother's voice in my head: "You have to take care of yourself so you have the energy to give to others."

I turned to see who was in the elevator with me, but I was alone. I smiled at my own actions, as I wondered where that voice came from. I realized I needed to listen to my own mom's words of advice and sat down at a table and ate some lunch. When I returned to Lindsey's room, she was still asleep and didn't even know I was gone.

> *Take care of yourself so you have the strength to give to others.*

As Lindsey started to get back her strength, I realized how scary it would have been if I had not kept asking questions at Urgent Care. I thought about how much the first pediatric doctor's words helped me. *I* knew my child. *I* knew she was in trouble, and I kept asking questions until I was heard.

I continued to develop confidence to ask questions when I wasn't sure what the doctor was explaining to me. I can even remember a time when I was leaving the pediatrician's office and I turned around and went back in. I asked to talk to him again, waited, and asked for clarification on what he said. I did that because as I started to walk out the door, that first pediatrician's words went through my head.

As I continued to challenge the medical staff, I

learned to use phrases like, "for MY child that's not normal."

By making it personal for *my* child, they were not able to tell me this was normal, even if it was for most children. I didn't threaten them that they didn't know what they were talking about (even if that is how I was feeling at the time). I felt like I was treated with more respect when I would say, "I am worried about . . ." or, "What do I look for next?"

In the Rearview Mirror of Feeling Like an Intern

Looking back, I remember experienced moms making jokes about how they could tell Danielle was my first because with your first child, moms are typically over protective, they have their children on a schedule, and they jump each time their child cries. I would get annoyed, thinking, I am NOT like that. I am an older mom and I don't overreact. It wasn't until I had three girls that I truly understood what they were saying. I was with a first time mom and she was acting the part. I realized I had changed my mothering behavior. I wasn't like she was, but I used to be. I explained to this new mom. "With my first baby, when her pacifier fell on the floor, I give her the spare from her diaper bag, just like you did. Then when it happened again, I would go wash off both pacifiers with hot water. With the second, I would take the pacifier and wipe it off on my pants. If I had a spare one in the bag, I couldn't find it. With the third, I would put it right back in her mouth or if it looked dirty, I would put it in my mouth first!"

The new mom was shocked and thought she would never do that. I joked and said, "Then you should only have one child."

I knew being a mom would be emotional. What I didn't anticipate was the rollercoaster of emotions I would have. The feelings were just so intense. The deep love and joy overflowed my heart. Total frustration would boil over with my inability to comfort my child. The feeling of complete exhaustion would overtake me from ever getting more than two hours of sleep in a row. However, just like riding a rollercoaster, the thrill of being a mom was worth the ride.

It goes without saying that I needed the love and support of my extended family. They were there to lend a helpful hand whenever I needed it and sometimes even read my mind from across the country. They had the right balance of offering suggestions without being judgmental, and Dan's parents always gave me positive reinforcement on my role as a mom. I was so lucky.

Why is it we say 'share' to our children when they play with others? Do they really share their toys? Or are we asking them to take turns? The two concepts are actually very different. There are times I taught the girls to share a toy, like the large play-kitchen, where one girl would be on one side, and the other girl on the other side. Then they would actually play together, being creative and cooperative. However, most of the time I taught the girls to take turns. When they had a toy, they could play with it until they were done, but then it was the next girl's turn. I wanted them to stand up for themselves, so when they got a new toy, they didn't have to share it right away. It could be their special toy.

I don't want to suggest that every parent needs to be a part of every medical procedure. I agree that most of the time, it is best to do as the doctors and nurses suggest. They are the ones with the training and experience. I would never want the nurse to have to leave my child's side to take care of me because I freaked out during a procedure. It was something I knew I could handle and I knew it would be important to my child if I was there. So I pushed to be there.

As a mom, I was constantly reminded many times that the only thing that stayed the same in parenting was that just when I had it figured out, things changed.

Chapter 5:
Full Time Mom

If our family was a business partnership, Dan would be the CFO and I would be the CEO. Like any business partnership, the CFO and CEO decide the goals (focus) of the business (family). The financial stability of the company rested solely on Dan as the CFO. As the CEO, I dealt with the day-to-day operations of the family. We both focused on the success of the family, but judged that success in different ways. For Dan, success was the ability to afford to do the things we wanted and save for the future. For me, success was happiness (morale) and daily achievements. Each role and end result was vitally important for our family, just like in a business partnership. These roles are interconnected, but they were not constructed like the hierarchy of a business. We communicated the overall focus of the family together and didn't operate without the support and encouragement of the other. Our family needed the CFO to focus on the financial success of the family so that the CEO could focus on the day-to-day operations. These separate roles with mutual support and respect were the keys to our family's success.

As the CEO Mommy, I was the most important person in the day-to-day operations of our children's lives. I was the one who they would go to when they were hurt. I could fix so much with just a hug. I could pass on encouragement with just a smile. I was able to support my girls as they worked through all of the stages of development, and sometimes that support was just being there. In the same way, Dan, the CFO, supported and encouraged me.

My Title

Every mom stays home with her newborn to recover from the birth of the child and adjust to the new demands of an infant in the family. The question that is asked before the child is even born is, "How long are you off of work?" Sometimes the question is even more personal: "How much paid time do you get?"

Each time I was asked these questions, I struggled. First of all, it was none of their business, especially if they were not a close friend or family member. Since I was taking paid maternity leave, I couldn't share publicly my intent not to return to work. So I would either try to totally avoid answering the question, or I would say, "We will see how things go."

Once I was able to tell people my plans to stay home with my child and not return to work, everyone was very supportive. They knew the job I had before becoming a mom was very demanding and didn't fit easily into having a young family, so most people expected I would quit. In addition, Dan was finishing school and was starting his new employment. Then our family continued to grow, so staying at home with them was an easy decision. Each time we had another child, friends, family, and even the public supported my role to stay home with them. Sometimes I would even joke that was why they were so close together— so I could return to work faster.

> *Be your true self and don't let social norms or lack of a title persuade you.*

I personally *loved* being a mom, but I struggled with a title. Whenever I was asked the question, "What do you do?" I didn't want to say, *'housewife'* . . . my role was a mother. I never liked having the house, *a building*, as part of my title. It seemed whenever I would try to say, *'stay at home mom,'* I would add in the word *'just'* so it would come across as, *'JUST a stay at home mom.'* But that is not how I felt; I felt it was a full-time job. That was when I realized my title was Full-time Mom. I loved it because it was what I was doing— focusing on being a mom— full-time. It was my new career; one that Dan and I decided would work for us. Eventually, I would even correct others if they used any of the other two titles for me. I was fairly stubborn about that.

I didn't realize that with the job title of Full-time Mom, I was giving other moms who had outside employment an attitude. They would often say, "I am a full-time mom, too," or "I am still a mom, even if I am working outside of the house."

I would just nod with half-hearted agreement, but I

knew we were different. It was a constant discussion in the 1990s. Most of our mothers had stayed at home and didn't work outside of the house; if they did, it was later in our childhood and within careers that fit easily with having a family. My generation of women had pushed for different professional careers and equal rights in the workplace. Women my age were respected for doing it all: having full careers *and* family. I had never thought that meant that I no longer could choose to be home with our children, full-time. I was shocked that the feeling of our society was that a truly liberated woman was a failure if they weren't employed outside of the home. 'I was a failure,' was the judgment that was shared with me often! Because of that, I am sure that I had an attitude in my voice when I would say I was a full-time mom, even though I respected the rights of others to choose to have a career and a family.

Coworkers and Training

When I was no longer employed outside of the home, I realized the thing I missed the most was going out to lunch with coworkers and participating in training. I was able to quickly figure out how to gain knowledge. I read many books and articles in magazines on childcare and the stages my girls were going through. I gathered information from as many different sources as possible, as there was no Internet yet.

After our move to Rochester, Dan realized I would need to get connected, and without employment he knew that would be hard. So he helped me get together with a couple of the wives of his coworkers who were each staying home with their first child. We decided to start a playgroup that met once a week. I was able to have adult conversations with Nancy and Melissa while our kids 'played' together. It seemed very strange to be in a playgroup when my daughter didn't even crawl yet, but it was what I needed. It was a chance to learn from other moms just by watching how they interacted with their children. It was also where I could ask for advice without judgment and even share my opinions.

We had a spin-off playgroup that was started from other coworkers of Dan's who had children and heard about the group. In addition, moms would invite other friends to come and they would also join us. This group would meet every other week at a park or at someone's house. I loved the social connection; it was like these stay at home moms were my coworkers.

Through this group, I learned about PAIIR (Parents Are Important In Rochester) educational classes for families of young children, and I started attending them. It was the training I was missing! PAIIR was a well-established program based on the age of the child. Each class started with parent/child activity time. Then I left Danielle with early childhood staff while I went to another classroom. I participated in a discussion group with a parent-educator who focused on development and age-related concerns. At the end of the class, all the moms would return to their children and we would gather around a circle and sing a few songs before we headed home. It was here that I learned the words and actions to the kids' song, "The Wheels on the Bus," and it is also where I met Peggy, who was new to town and had a daughter Danielle's age. She joined our small playgroup. The four of us – Peggy, Nancy, Melissa and I – continued to meet one morning a week. Not only did our children grow, but so did our friendships. We were able to trust in each other with the ups and downs of motherhood and even swapped childcare.

I continued my *'training'* with the PAIIR classes by signing up for the appropriate age class for Danielle each semester. After Ashley was born, I was able to take her into the classroom with me as I learned and discussed with the other moms. When I had Lindsey, Dan and I led an infant class one evening a week for eight weeks. I was still attending a class one morning a week with a focus on two-year-olds, while Ashley went to sibling care and Lindsey stayed with me.

Now my job as a full-time mom felt complete, with each day filled with caring for three little girls. I was connected to *'coworkers'* with two different playgroups that were meeting about six times a month. The thing I missed from working outside of the home was lunch with coworkers. Now I had that with our playgroup. I continued to receive the *'training for my job'* at the PAIIR classes. I was focused on doing my best at my job as a full-time mom.

> *It is important not to be an island. Be sure to connect with other parents!*

Job Searching

After Lindsey turned one, people began asking me when I would be going back to work. It seemed like a reasonable question from family members or very close friends, but I was shocked that it was a common question from complete strangers. I started hearing it so much that I started to wonder if it was time for a change. *Was staying home with my children still the right thing for me to do?*

Danielle would be starting preschool, and the idea had been tossed out enough in my social circle that one day I compared myself to my neighbor who had outside employment. This mom had a three-year-old daughter, and at that time, this was how old Ashley was, too. In the morning, I watched her leave for work, carrying her daughter with her to drop her off at day care. I was just coming down the stairs with Ashley, who had just woken up and was still in her pajamas. I had already been up with Danielle and given her a quick morning snack, and had said goodbye to Dan as he headed off to work. Lindsey was still in bed, sound asleep. I thought about how happy I was that I didn't have to have anyone dressed yet . . . not even myself.

While my neighbor was at work, we had breakfast, got dressed, watched Sesame Street, went to the park, had snacks at the park, came home for lunch, the girls had nap time, I paid bills, after naps they had another snack, and I started supper while the girls played Pretend Pool. (Pretend Pool is to take all of the couch cushions and set them on the floor in front of the couch.

They become the pool. The couch is now the side of the pool. Then they jumped into the pool onto the cushions.) As I walked back into the living room to check on the girls, I saw the neighbor mom return home and get her daughter out of the car. As I looked at my active girls – now pretending to walk on rocks so they would not fall into lava – I felt a rush of contentment. I knew for me this was right where I needed to be; for my family, this fit perfectly. I had the confidence to once again fight the judgment of others.

Yet, I felt like I should be contributing to the family budget, and I had a sense that Dan, the CFO, wouldn't have minded. Like most families, we could use more money, so I asked Dan how much his co-workers were paying for day care. Using that information, I realized I was saving the family a lot of money each week because we were not paying for childcare for three. I may not have been bringing money into the budget, but without paying for childcare for three children, we were ahead financially.

As I looked into the future, I realized that in a couple of years I would only have Lindsey left at home while the others were in preschool. I started to dream about teaching at the PAIIR (Parents Are Important In Rochester) community education classes. I figured I would be a great Parent Educator with all of my personal experience and college degree.

Job Transfer
That plan was derailed as life threw us a curveball.

Dan's employer was downsizing and many of these families were moving. It wasn't long before we made the decision to move across the country to Mesa, Arizona. We were leaving the town where Ashley and Lindsey were born; we were leaving our home. I was going to be separated from my *'coworkers,' 'training,'* and the tentative future I had started to dream about. I had to find some strength to deal with it all and help my girls adjust to these changes, so I started telling them this story:

"Once upon a time, there was a family with three girls that were going on an adventure. The Daddy got a new job in a new state and had to leave the family to start his new job. The Mommy was busy keeping the house clean and taking care of the girls; Danielle was four years old, Ashley was about to celebrate her third birthday, and Lindsey was 18 months old. Soon, hopefully very soon, their house would sell to another family. Then the Daddy could come for a visit to help the Mommy and the girls move. A big truck would come and load up all of the things from the house, even the toys, but the girls each kept their special blankies in their own hands (the girls' would grab their blankies). The next day, the family would fly in an airplane to start their adventure.

First, they would stay in the Daddy's apartment while they brought their new house. One day, the big moving truck would come with all of the family's furniture and toys in it. All of it would be moved into their new home. The Daddy, the Mommy, and three girls would live happily ever after."

The first time I told the story, I think it was more for my own adjustment, reminding myself that there was a happy ending. This story became a favorite story for me to tell the girls, especially Ashley. I added in details as plans were getting finalized. When things actually started to happen, they would look up at me and say, "Mommy, it is just like the story!"

After six weeks, we were all tired of living apart so we started on our adventure. The house would sell without us living there. We couldn't wait to be together as a family any longer (actually, Dan just missed us too much). The moving company arrived to pack up all of our stuff. One of my *'coworkers,'* Peggy, and her daughter, Marie, stopped by with lunch for the girls and me. We ended up sitting on the floor in the kitchen, eating, as it was the only place to stay out of the way. I wanted to at least pay Peggy for lunch since I wouldn't be able to buy her lunch in the future. She said no, and told me to pay it forward to someone else in need at my new location. Peggy taught me the importance of just helping out others when I could, not for repayment. As I needed to lean on others in the beginning of our adventure, I remembered Peggy and the pay it forward thought. (This is way before the pay it forward movement.) I knew that right then I was the one in need, but in the future I would be able to pay it forward to help someone else. In the end, it all worked out. I didn't realize how strong these relationships had become until the day I had to say goodbye. I felt sadness that the girls would not be growing up with these friends like I had envisioned, which brought tears to my eyes.

As the tears flowed down my face, Danielle asked, "Will we would be visiting them again?"

"We will see," was all I could say, but I knew we would most likely never see these people again. Not only were we moving, but most of them were relocating to different places in the United States as well. Tears continued to stream down my face. After the sadness, I felt a total emptiness as I realized I was losing my lifeline as a stay at home mom. I began sobbing. I wasn't sure how I would adjust or survive without their support. I was glad I was driving home in the dark and the girls were too little to realize my sadness.

The busyness of the move helped filled space where my loneliness would have lived. An answer for my adult connection was found on our very first Sunday in Arizona. In

The big move from MN to AZ

the church bulletin, they had advertised a playgroup that met regularly at a park on Tuesday mornings. We attended that Tuesday and I started to build relationships with the moms at that playgroup. Tentatively but with determination, I realized that I would survive. It wasn't long after I started attending this playgroup that I needed to have someone watch my girls while I dealt with some details from our move. I asked one of the friendliest and attentive moms – Becky – if any of them had ever swapped babysitting. Becky said they hadn't but she didn't mind helping me out. The girls and I went to her house early so all of us could get comfortable. It wasn't long before the girls were playing with her son or having fun on their own. I felt very comfortable with her. So off I went for a few hours, only calling her to check on the girls three times. When I picked them up, I thanked her many times and reminded her that it was now my turn to watch her son when she needed a break or had an appointment. To this day, I don't know what I would have done without her help and support. We supported each other and our roles as stay at home moms and became very good friends.

The adjustment to our new location had gone very well. I had found *'coworkers'* with the playgroup, a preschool for Danielle, and dance classes for both Ashley and Danielle. Now the other thing I really wanted to find was a place to get my *'training,'* a parent-child education outlet. I remember the day I started calling around and looking for something similar to what I had in Rochester. After the third call, I realized what I was asking and how it sounded to the people at the other end. I sounded like a desperate mom who was overwhelmed with her children. I was starting to worry if the people at the other end of the phone were going to call in Social Services, so I decided I better drop that search. It would be another year until I learned about some parenting class at the local elementary school. I did attend them and met some other awesome moms. However, these parenting classes were not as good as the first ones I took.

My Work Routine

I liked variety and really didn't enjoy doing the same thing at the same time every day. Even though I had realized the importance of a nighttime schedule and routine, I didn't translate that into my *'work day'* very quickly. Accidently, I had established a lunch break in my *'work day.'* It started when the girls were infants and fell asleep after being fed; that's when I would get a break. As they started having solid foods, they were awake for a longer period of time and their sleep patterns moved to morning and afternoon naps. The morning nap would just sort of happen, but the afternoon nap fell right after lunch. I would clean them up from their messy lunch, change them, and lay them down for a nap. That gave me time to go back to the kitchen and clean up the mess. Then it was a great time for me to sit down and relax. It didn't take long before the girls' afternoon nap was set around a soap opera I liked to watch, so before 1:00 p.m. each day, the girls were in their beds having a nap. I had my hour to watch my soap opera and relax. After my soap opera break, I was able to take care of other household tasks before they would begin to wake up from their afternoon naps. I, too, was refreshed.

The morning naps didn't happen at the same time each day and as the girls got older there were mornings they didn't take a nap. Every day that happened, our morning would be crazy. Sometimes we would go to the park, sometimes we would have a friend over, sometimes Dan would come home for lunch, and other days we just stayed home. The stay at home mom flexibility I was enjoying was stressing everyone out.

When Danielle started preschool, I was pushed into a morning routine that helped everyone. Ashley, especially, was calmer knowing what was happening each day. It wasn't long before each *'work day'* had a routine. On Monday and Friday mornings we took Danielle to preschool and Ashley, Lindsey, and I returned home to hang out. On Wednesday mornings we took Danielle to school and the three of us ran errands. On Tuesday mornings, the three girls and I went to playgroup in the park. On Thursday mornings, Ashley and Danielle had dance class.

We even fell into a routine on what we did during our dance time. While Ashley was in dance class, Danielle, Lindsey, and I went to the bagel store just around the corner from the dance studio. Each girl had half a plain bagel and juice, since I wasn't about to have them spilling cream cheese or butter all over themselves. When Ashley was done, she would get her half a bagel and eat it while we waited for Danielle in the dance studio. Sometimes we needed to pick up a few groceries, so we would walk down a little farther to the grocery store. At the grocery store, the bakery would give kids a free cookie, so that was their treat instead of a bagel, and I would purchase a cookie for Ashley to eat later. We would grab the groceries and hurry back to the dance studio in time to switch girls. Then we would load the car, return the cart to the grocery store, and head back to the dance studio as Danielle was finishing up. These were things that just happened, but soon turned into my *'work routine.'*

> *Routine is comforting to some personalities and provides structure for everyone.*

After our treasured afternoon naps, the girls would play until everyone woke up. Then they would have an afternoon snack time. A way to encourage their independence with their food choices started with their snacks. I had a basket of individually packaged snacks. They could go to that basket and pick their own snack. To save money, I didn't always buy pre-packaged snacks, but we made our own using snack-sized re-sealable bags. After a trip to the grocery store, I would open a box of animal crackers or cheese-flavored crackers and count out an exact number and put them into a snack bag. I wasn't surprised when the girls thought their bag was smaller than their sisters. They started to line them up to compare! Then I would teach them to count them to compare. It was great practice. It wasn't long before they were helping *me* put together the snack bags and counting up the crackers. Then, if the bags were not exactly even, I would just say, "Maybe someone had a taste when they were putting them in the bag."

After snack time, the girls would play until about 5 o'clock . . . then we would hit the disaster time of the day. It was the time of the day when three things collided at once: the end of my patience, the kids' hungry/cranky time, and time for me to be working on dinner. I called it, 'D time', which, for me, meant Disaster Time! But the girls thought the 'D' meant it was almost time for 'Daddy' to come home.

If I was lucky, I would get them settled and watching *The Magic School Bus*[2] or another PBS show before 'D time' would hit. As soon as the show started, I would rush around in the kitchen to get as much of the dinner prep done as possible. Hopefully, Dan would be home shortly after that. If not, we would all just try to survive until he arrived. (I always wondered if Dan thought my whole day was just like 'disaster time.')

When the girls were young, we always sat around the kitchen table to eat supper together. About once a week, usually on Sundays, we would eat in the dining room. This was the time for them to learn how to use their good manners. There were many times I wondered why we went through all of the work. We had to take a plastic tablecloth, lay it on the carpet, put Lindsey's high chair on it and move Ashley's booster-seat. As we ate, I would say a silent prayer that we could get through the meal without any liquids being spilled, but I believed the girls had to practice to learn how to eat at restaurants.

After dinner, if the weather was nice, it was time to play outside; it was the best way to wear the girls out. We would take walks, play in the back yard, on the swings, or play tag. It was fun to see all the crazy ideas the girls would come up with. When the weather wasn't good, we would try to do something inside, but of course there were times when we would end up watching TV. We ended our daily routine with baths, individual time for one of us to read them books, and both of us would tuck them into bed each night.

The next day, we would repeat the whole *'work day'* routine again. As they got older and many of their peers were giving up naps, I started to feel guilty about my continued routine. *Was I putting my personal desires above the needs of my children?* They were still able to go to bed at night on time, so it wasn't like their naps were affecting their sleep. But was I forcing a nap just for my soap opera? Then I read, *'When mothers never take care of their needs, they are teaching their daughters that a woman's needs are not important. When a mother demonstrates that they have needs and that those needs are as important as their children or husbands, then they are teaching their daughters that they are important.'* I was, in fact, teaching my daughters that a woman's needs were important. I even started calling it *Mommy Time for Mommy*! This routine continued even when the girls were elementary school age and didn't nap anymore. Each day in the summer after lunch, they went up to their rooms for quiet time. They didn't sleep anymore and were too old for naps, but they were content with quiet time. Each girl would be in her room, reading a book on her own. (That might be why all three of them are still avid readers.)

There were times they would fall asleep, and other times they would be playing quietly in their rooms, but I pretended not to hear. The point was this was their time to be on their own and for me to have Mommy Time for Mommy.

> *Taking care of yourself is not selfish.*

Weekends

On weekends, we struggled to balance the chores and repairs around the house with family fun time. At last I realized how nice routines were for our family during the week; I thought that a weekend schedule might be helpful, too, so we started taking turns as parents, switching off who was the parent-in-charge of the girls, or who was given time to focus on their needs or to-do-list. So one Saturday, I would be the parent-in-charge and Dan would have time to focus on what he wanted to get done. Sometimes he would take one child along with him to the hardware store, or just run the errand on his own. But that was his choice; I was in charge of the girls. (It was always easy to take one child compared to three.) I would focus on the girls and keep them on their routine. They could see what Daddy was doing, but I would keep them out of his hair while he focused on getting something done.

The next weekend we would switch roles. I would do a major project, or go to lunch with a friend, without kids. Daddy was the parent-in-charge. Of course the girls would get confused and come to me and ask me questions, but I would just remind them, "It's Daddy's day; go ask him."

When the girls were six, seven, and eight years old, I realized it was time to have them help out more around the house. It was time for *everyone* to have a cleaning job, so we started to have a clean-up day in our house. Since Dan was going to be a part of clean-up day, he chose to do the vacuuming. If Dan had a chore, he wanted to do it first thing on Saturday morning. He wanted to get started right away and be done so he could get on to other things or enjoy his day. Since the girls' job was to pick up their rooms good enough for Dan to vacuum, they headed up to do their rooms right after breakfast. They would begin to pick up their toys and then start to play with them. When Dan would get to their rooms to vacuum, there would be more toys on the floor than before they started! He would get frustrated and try to hurry them along. He was getting mad that it was taking them forever. The girls didn't like doing their job and were just getting yelled at. At some point, Dan would finally get a chance to get their rooms vacuumed sometime on Saturday, but by Sunday night the rooms were disasters again. This plan was not working!

I suggested to Dan that he should use Saturday mornings to do other things he wanted to get done around the house. Then on Sunday afternoons he could do the vacuuming. He wasn't excited about doing it on Sunday, but he knew what we were doing now didn't work. So the girls still headed upstairs to pick up their room after breakfast on Saturdays, but they had until lunch time on Sunday to be done. At first they thought they had to work on it all that time, but I pointed out it could take them half an hour and then they could play . . . it just had to be ready for Daddy to vacuum by Sunday afternoon. They would spend all morning in their rooms, clean a little, play a lot . . . clean a little, play a lot. There were times this would continue into the afternoon on Saturday. It ended up being a great way to have a relaxing weekend. The girls were doing their chores their way, so it didn't seem like such a job, and Dan was patient because he was able to get something else done on Saturday mornings. Of course, every once in a while I would look under the beds and make them clean up all the stuff they had hidden there over the past several weeks. They weren't happy with me when I did that, but I knew it needed to be done.

> *If at first you don't succeed, remind yourself of the big picture and try again.*

On Sunday after rest/quiet time, we would remind the girls that Daddy was going to vacuum their rooms so they would have to pick up their things. It worked great the first few weekends, but it wasn't long before someone left too many toys out and wasn't ready for Daddy to vacuum. Dan started getting frustrated again and the girls were getting yelled at. Our relaxing Sunday was no longer relaxing and it wasn't how I wanted our weekend to end. It was obvious that yelling wasn't working— we needed better consequences. Instead of focusing on the one that wasn't done, we rewarded whoever *was* done with a family movie, popcorn, and soda pop. There were times when one or all of the girls wouldn't get their rooms cleaned, so they would hear the movie and smell the popcorn, but they couldn't be a part of the movie time if they hadn't finished their job. Once they were done, they could come join us for the movie. If someone really didn't get their room vacuumed one week, it wasn't the end of the world. Most of the time they were ready and there wasn't any more yelling on Sunday afternoons.

As the girls got older, they even asked if they could vacuum their own rooms. Now Dan didn't have to wait until Sunday afternoon to do his job. The new rule in the house was that their rooms had to be cleaned and vacuumed by supper on Sunday night. They could do it earlier in the weekend, but it had to be done by then. There were many times when the girls were in junior high they had things they wanted to do on the weekend. They just knew to clean their rooms before they even asked if they could head to a friend's house to play. Cleaning their rooms every week was just part of their routine!

Commuting: Car Rides
With all of the girls' activities, we spent a great deal of time in the car. I never understood why being in the car

would bring out the worst behavior in the girls. Having everyone buckled into a tight space and sometimes touching each other was the real problem.

Car trip craziness

One day, I was not able to concentrate on driving on the four-lane city road because of what was going on in the back seat. While I was looking into my rear view mirror, I hit the car in front of me. He had decided to stop at a red light. It was just a bumper-to-bumper thing, so there was no damage, but of course, my angel child, Ashley, said to Dan that night, "Mommy hit a car."

I quickly used this as a teaching opportunity . . . or at least to make sure Dan knew the whole story! I asked Ashley why that happened.

"Because you didn't stop," her three-year-old voice squeaked out.

"Why do you think I didn't stop?" I asked.

"Exactly what I want to know," Dan commented under his breath.

"Because you were going too fast," Ashley said.

Before this whole thing got out of hand, I decided I better explain. "I wasn't looking at the car in front of me Ashley. I had to look in the mirror because someone was crying, someone else was hitting them, and someone else was yelling. And just then the car in front of me stopped, and I didn't see it. So I have decided that I need to concentrate on driving, and you girls have to be better riders, starting tomorrow."

Dan decided to share his concern, "Great idea . . . I can't wait to hear how it works out tomorrow."

The next day, a similar moment arose in the back seat. Without hesitation, I took an immediate right and then parked. I turned around and addressed the girls. "Remember yesterday when Mommy bumped that car? I did it because you were not being good riders and I took my eyes off the road in front of me to deal with you. I can't do that anymore; it is not safe."

They all looked scared, but I continued to explain. "So from now on, when you misbehave in the car I am going to do what I did today. I am going to pull over and stop. But next time, whoever is causing the trouble is going to get a time out on the curb. Does anyone need a time-out now?"

They all shook their heads and agreed they could be good. And for the rest of that trip they were. But later in the day, they forgot and once again someone was distracting me. So I took the next right, pulled over to the curb, and parked. I got out of the car, walked around to the passenger side, and opened the back door of the minivan. I unbuckled Lindsey from her car seat. She was so scared because she wasn't sure what was going to happen. She yelled, "I'll be good!"

I didn't say anything as I set her on the curb. I sat on the edge of the van with the door open right next to her. The other two yelled, "Don't leave her!"

Seriously, where do kids get these ideas?

After just a minute, I asked Lindsey if she was ready to behave. She quickly nodded as I put her back into her car seat.

This turned out to be a great solution, because sometimes, I needed time to cool off, too. The whining and crying from the backseat could be so distracting. It was good to remind myself to focus on my driving. As a matter of fact, one really stressful day, I pulled over, parked the car, got out walked over to the curb and sat down. *I* needed a time out. I could hear the girls crying, so I only sat on the curb for a minute. As I got back into the car I said, "Mommy needed a time out. She wasn't being good."

> *Distracted driving, no matter what the cause, is dangerous, especially with your most precious cargo– your children– in the car.*

The last time I needed to do this was with Ashley, who was deathly afraid of dogs. Without realizing it, I had pulled over right next to a fence with a dog just on the other side. Just as I was about to set her on the curb, the dog started barking. You could even see his little nose through the fence. Ashley was totally freaked out. I didn't even release my hands from her shoulders, even though if you ask her she says I left her there forever. I hugged her and put her back into her car seat. She decided she would NEVER cause me to stop again. She would even remind her sisters when they would start to misbehave, "You don't want Mommy to stop do you?" All it would take would be slowing down, or taking a quick right turn, and they would pipe up. "Mommy, I'll be good."

Promotion: Time for a Real Job

When the girls were young, I believed I would return to some type of employment once they were in school. From many discussions we had, I knew that Dan truly thought I would, also. Before our first big move, I thought I would become a parent educator at PAIIR, but it wasn't meant to be! At least I hadn't just started working there when we had to move.

I think Dan thought I would go back to teaching since that would fit so nicely into the girls' schedule. I had done that years before we met and just didn't have the desire to return to teaching; it just didn't feel like a fit for me anymore. But what would I do for a *'real'* job? When would be a good time for me do start a *'real'* job?

As Danielle started first grade, I was there to put her on the bus in the morning, and was there when she returned each day. During the time she was gone, I was still busy with the same routine with Ashley and Lindsey. When Danielle would return from school each day, she would sit down for her afternoon snack and share the details of her day. Later when Dan would get home from work, he would ask Danielle about her day, and she would say it was fine. At supper we would discuss our days and when I would ask her about one of the stories she told me, she would remember and share, but I noticed she had lost the emotions of the day. I realized there was still a benefit for me to be home for her when she got off the school bus. In addition, I was able to volunteer at her school and was there when she was home sick. As I looked ahead to when all the girls would be in elementary school, and I was sure I wanted to have the ability to be there for them, somehow.

I started to test the waters of having a *'real'* job by expanding my volunteer roles. I learned about small group ministry and worked on implementing that into our church offerings. One of the things I helped implement was a Parenting Class which met one evening a week and for which I was the group leader. I really enjoyed it, but as a family we struggled to make it work. One night every week, Dan had to leave work at a certain time so he could be home in time for me to leave for my volunteer job. With Dan's position at the time, it just didn't work. We decided it wasn't a good option for us at this stage of our family. It was just too stressful.

I continued to search for more options, focusing first on the flexibility we needed for our family. I wanted to be home in the morning until the girls were on the school bus and be able to be home in the afternoon when they got off the school bus. I wanted to continue to volunteer at the girls' school, and would need flexibility to be home when the girls were sick. It seemed like outside employment – even part-time – would just add too much stress to an already stressful family. But I kept thinking and searching for the right answer.

When Lindsey was in her last year of preschool, I decided I would like to have my own business so I could control my schedule. I had many ideas for starting my own business, but I didn't think I had the business skills, I wasn't sure how to even begin, and the details felt overwhelming . . . then I discovered direct sales. It was exactly what I wanted. It gave me the flexibility to schedule my events around our family schedule. I could plan most of the events on Saturdays when Dan would be home. I could host many things in our home, so if Dan was late, I could still be ready for my event. My customers were going to be other mothers so they would understand interruptions from my children.

Being in direct sales was the answer for me. I enjoyed the connection with other adults and the flexibility of planning things around the girls' schedule. I had already fallen in love with the products from the company I would be representing and had a group of women who were in love with them, too. The added benefit was that I would be able to get my supplies at-cost. Actually, most of the profit of the business went back into my business, so my customers were actually purchasing my products for my 'personal hobby.' That was the problem Dan had with it; it was not an income-producer, and it wasn't really adding to the family income.

> *Finding life balance becomes a priority, even over status and income.*

But that was just not a priority for me. I enjoyed the recognition that being involved in direct sales offered me. As I got more successful, I even made a good friend of mine, Sandy, my assistant. (I paid her with products.) She was able watch the kids until Dan got home if I had an event on a week night. Being in direct sales was my answer to the question *'What do you do?'* that I was still being asked.

In the Rearview Mirror of Full-Time Mom

Looking back, I loved my opportunity to be a Full-time Mom. I realize that my role as a mom was more treasured because I spent so much time anticipating that I may not become a mother. So staying at home to be with the girls full-time was something I just felt compelled to do. I recognize not everyone has that option; many families need both parents to work to make ends meet. But I have also witnessed many people who choose a lifestyle that demands both parents work, and that is a choice that I respect. I just hope they respect the choices of others who decide that parenting full-time, whether they are a full-time mom or a full-time dad, is their priority. When I first decided to stay at home with Danielle, I didn't decide it would be forever. It just ended up that way with the twists and turns of my life. I enjoyed having the flexibility of working from home and keeping the family my main focus.

Being a mom was just like any other job. It was very important to learn not only through experience, but also from others. I found the best teachers to be other moms.

They had the best ideas that worked for one child or another. Being able to find parenting classes should be easy. Moms shouldn't have to fear they are going to be reported to Department of Social Services just for asking.

Every time I heard the flight attendant go over this emergency safety rule, "When the oxygen masks appear put your mask on first then help your child," I'd think, no way would I do that. I would put my child's on first! Now I realize we would both be dead. By the time I put the mask on my struggling child, I would pass out. If I would do as the rule says, put my mask on first, my child would see it on me, not be as scared, and I would have oxygen to fight with them. Life as a mom is just like that oxygen mask metaphor. You have to take time for yourself so you have the 'oxygen' to help your child. Without taking time to recharge yourself, you both will run out of energy.

Chapter 6:
My Role as a Manager

I understood that my role was to manage the girls and their unique personality traits. I knew that those personalities would come from both Dan and me. Dan and I are quite the opposite, so I anticipated a variety of traits would be present in the girls. I could easily understand and relate to the traits that were like my own . . . *most* of the time, and I didn't think about how some of Dan's personality traits in a child could drive me crazy. I learned to be creative in my managing style, but there were times when I would just say to Dan, "You go deal with her, she is acting like you."

As I set the boundaries and standards for the girls, I started to realize that I expected them to react to situations as I did. I wanted them to behave as I would. Then all of a sudden, I realized I was turning them all into little Loris. Now that is a scary thought! Just like on a job, each person doesn't handle a situation exactly the same. I had to step back and let them react in their own ways and guide them only when needed. I couldn't expect that the girls would react the same way; I had to adjust my own personality traits and responses to their unique traits. For example, I am more of a go-with-the-flow type person, but that drove Dan– who likes to have a plan–

crazy. Being part of this family meant I had to be willing to give and take.

Opposite Projects

Once I was home with (baby) Ashley, some things were easier because I wasn't a new mom; I had done this before. But I learned that each child was different. Many of the techniques that worked with Danielle didn't work with Ashley. I discovered that Ashley loved to be bundled up. She seemed to have a cranky time at the end of the day. She liked to be rocked quickly in the rocking chair or to be walked. But at a certain time of the night it was anyone's guess. I would try walking her, feeding her, changing her, rocking her, and then pass her to Dan who would repeat all of the above. What worked one night didn't seem to work the next night. One night as I went through my list of things to try I was getting increasing frustrated. I knew that would only make things worse, so I quickly laid her on the living room floor out of total aggravation. She stopped crying and looked up at me, as if to say, "Thank you."

It seemed she just wanted to be left alone. Everything I had been trying had to do with me touching her. She'd had enough touching! From that day on, laying her on the floor became a technique I used to soothe her. Many times I felt bad leaving her there all alone, so I would lie down next to her and just be by her side. She liked that unless I got too huggy. I quickly learned she was very different from Danielle.

I even remember my Mother telling me about my

older brothers and how they were opposites. When there was a problem with a piece of farm machinery, my brother, Butch, would walk around it a couple of times, thinking. My brother, Ed, would disappear for a minute and return with a hammer and start hitting the broken part. Sometimes Ed's method worked. When it didn't, Butch was ready to do what was needed because he had thought it out. There were times Butch would stop him and point out a different approach first. When they tried the thought-out idea, it usually worked. But if it didn't, Ed was ready with his hammer.

My brothers were opposites, just like my first two girls. I realized that what worked for one may not work for the other. Over time I switched to opposite techniques quicker and found success faster.

Juggling Projects: Every Child is Unique
When I was pregnant with my third child, I was so happy. I would truly know how to raise her because my first two were opposites. This one would be just like one of the other two and then I would know what to do. No one ever told me she could be totally unique. As much as two can be opposite, my three girls are different, like three equilateral triangles!

Lindsey loved to be held and comforted like Danielle did, but was also content to be left alone. I could even stop feeding her in the middle of a feeding if one of the other girls needed me at that moment. She would look up at me shocked that I had stopped, but would just wait. She didn't even cry and when I would return, she would continue eating. Yet, she loved to sleep on my stomach to feel close to me. So she was equally different than the other two. I had a lot to learn as the three unique girls grew!

Unique Girls: Danielle, Lindsey, and Ashley

Danielle would be ready to go sleep at her bedtime no matter where we were. If we were out late, she would climb on my lap, put her head on my shoulder, and fall asleep. She would stay asleep or go right back to sleep as we moved her to the car and into her bed. She was always an early bird, and even if we were able to keep her up late, she would be up at her usual time the next morning—only she would be cranky for not getting enough sleep. (We learned not to do that often.)

Conversely, Lindsey loved to keep going. She didn't like to stop at bedtime. If we were out late, she was up late; nothing would stop her. She would have been a night owl if I had let her. If she went to sleep late at night, she would sleep later in the morning. Her bedtime routine helped her calm down and fall asleep.

What works for one child will more than likely not work for another!

Ashley liked her bed and would fall right to sleep when she was laid in her bed. She wanted me to put her down, to be left alone, and to go to sleep on her own, which was great for when we were home, but not when we were out and about. I finally realized she would fall asleep with movement. I could get her to calm down by walking with her or pushing her in the stroller. In the car, she would sleep until the car stopped. She also didn't like her schedule changed. When she was really little she started falling asleep before 7:00 p.m. and Dan would hardly see her. Once she even fell asleep before supper because I was trying to keep her up. No matter what I did, I couldn't keep her up, until the ending of day light savings time. Ashley's schedule included waking up about the same time every day, no matter what time she went to sleep at night. If she didn't get to sleep on time at night, she was (predictably) very cranky. A sleep routine was a key for Ashley's happiness.

Even though they had totally different sleep patterns, they were all very good sleepers. For the most part, they slept through the night, except for the random nightmare. Danielle had the most violent nightmares, which were actually night terrors. She would cry out in the middle of the night with a bad dream, but wouldn't actually wake up. When I would come in to comfort her, I would become the scary person in her dream. After I realized they were night terrors, it seemed anything I did made it worse. It worked out better if Dan went to her and could wake her up as he comforted her. At first I thought it was just a phase. As they continued, I searched for answers. I tried to blame watching TV too close to bedtime. But it didn't always happen. Finally, I realized Danielle had night terrors on the nights we had watched Disney movies. It wasn't until years later when she was able to talk more did I find out it was a certain Disney movie—*101 Dalmatians*[3]. She was upset that the puppies were stolen but their blankie was left behind.

Watching movies before bed didn't bother Ashley, but the fire drill at school caused nightmares for her. At first I thought she would just get over it or get used to it. But she didn't. I started to talk to her about them, hoping to help her share her feelings. It seemed like she just didn't like to be reminded that bad things could happen. As I continued to think about how to help her, I realized that she was a three year old that had logic like a teenager. So I decided I would reason with her like I would a teenager. I was afraid I would make things worse, but I was willing to give it a try.

"If we have a fire, the fire alarm would keep us safe because we get outside safely. But the things in our house would be burned up in a fire." She started to cry but I continued. "So that is why we have insurance. If there was a fire in our house, our insurance would give us money to buy all the things that were lost in the fire."

"I don't want a new blankie or Dollie," she cried.

"Where is your blankie and Dollie?" I asked. She held them up as she was holding them. I continued, "Exactly! You always have blankie and Dollie with you so they would make it outside with you."

We continued to discuss all of the things that

My Role as a Manager

insurance would buy and how, with insurance, we were safe. It wasn't until the next day at breakfast when Ashley shared with her sisters all about insurance did I realize that she didn't have a nightmare and she wasn't scared of fire alarms any more.

I remember trying to comfort Ashley from a nightmare that didn't make sense. I kept saying to her that it was just a dream, but her logical mind couldn't understand how the people just showed up in her dream and why preschool teachers were in her house. It just didn't make sense. She wanted it to be logical. Finally out of frustration I said, "We are going to throw your bad dreams out the door. Put all of your bad dreams into your hands."

I helped her rub her face, chest, and tummy as we put her hands tightly together. I told her to hold them tight as I carried her down the stairs. I opened up the front door and helped her throw her hands open as if she was throwing something away. I quickly shut the front door and locked it.

I told her, "Now those bad dreams are gone and can't get back in." She smiled as I took her back up to bed.

> *Trying to understand toddlers is hard, but trying to comprehend a sleepy toddler is almost impossible. Stop trying to understand and just find a way to get through it.*

All three girls went through the 'scared of monsters' night time routine. I was never sure if they really were scared of something or if they were trying to put off bedtime. My parenting books gave some good advice. I put water in a spray bottle and labeled it, 'Monster Spray'. During the night, I would spray where they *saw* the monsters and the girls believed it worked. I would even give them the spray bottle to put by their bed to spray any monsters that might sneak back in after I left. It prevented me from having to come back and what harm could a little water do?

Lindsey loved to be creative and would make up dreams as a way to go to sleep. Sometimes as I would tuck her into bed she would say to me, "I can't think of any dreams to have so I won't be able to sleep."

I would brainstorm some ideas and soon she was ready to go to sleep. One year right after Easter, Lindsey (who was five at the time) had trouble going to sleep several nights in a row. At first I thought she was playing a game with me, so finally one night, I sat down with her and asked what was bothering her.

She said, "I don't want to die like Jesus."

I didn't want to say that she would die; everyone dies. I figured that wouldn't help my sleepless nights. So I went with, "Jesus is in heaven. Heaven is a good place to be."

She wasn't too convinced and said she wanted to know if her blankie would be in heaven. I didn't want to lie, and since I truly don't know, I said, "If you need your blankie, God will make sure it is there. God wants you to be happy and have everything you need in heaven."

She was satisfied and went off to bed. The next

morning she announced to her sisters that God would have their blankies in heaven. She was safe and happy, again. And I was happy I would have a full night's sleep until the next thing.

To-Do List
Ashley loved having a daily plan and didn't like to change it. Conversely, I am not one to write a to-do list, but I always know in my head what needs to happen each day. At breakfast as a preschooler, Ashley would ask, "What are we doing today?"

At first I would just tell her what activity we were doing. Then I recognized she wanted to know more. So I made it a teaching moment.

"It is Wednesday. What do we do on Wednesday?"

In the beginning, she didn't know the answer, but it didn't take long for her to know exactly what we did each morning on which day. She loved to know the answer just by knowing the day of the week. It made Ashley content knowing what was ahead; I would ask her, "Since it is Friday, what are we doing today?"

"We take Danielle to preschool and come back home to play until we pick her up," she said, happy that I had asked her this time.

"What do we do after we pick up Danielle from preschool?" I continued. She looked at me puzzled, so I explained, "What do we do in the middle of every day?"

"Lunch," she yelled excitedly.

"And then?" I continued to ask after each answer.

"Nap time, snacks, play, TV, Daddy comes home,

supper, play outside, bath, and bedtime." She finally got through the whole day.

"Exactly right. You know our whole day," I said to her as I gave her a hug.

"Thanks, Mommy," she would often reply with excitement as she would head off to play. It was comforting to Ashley to have a routine in her days.

Lindsey just liked being able to do anything outside of the house. She wasn't happy if we weren't going somewhere, but she didn't care about knowing in advance. I could always tell her when we would be going next. Of course since the girls are three unique individuals, Danielle liked the times we stayed home and had nothing to do. She didn't like to have to go somewhere every day; she just wanted to be home. I remember wondering how old she needed to be to be able to leave her at home so Lindsey, Ashley, and I could just keep going!

Controlling Your Attitude

How you feel is reflected out to others in your attitude. What I didn't know is that I would need to teach my girls how to deal with those feelings. Danielle was the content child who seemed to just go with the flow and not get upset, but she also had a limit. When she was a toddler, she would bite someone, throw toys at someone, and hit us. She would keep everything inside until she couldn't hold it in anymore and would then explode with unacceptable behavior. I had to teach her to hit the couch or a pillow when she was mad. I could see that she was keeping things to herself. I worked really hard to tell her to let her feelings out instead of hit things or other people. When she was feeling sad, she would love to climb on my lap for a hug. She would share her tears with me and talk out her sadness.

As Danielle grew, she kept many of her feelings inside and thought things through whenever possible. She would often go to her room when she was upset. I suppose she was trying to sort out her feelings, but it drove me nuts. I believed I was to notice that she was missing and go check on her. I would find her on her bed crying, waiting for me to ask, "What's wrong?" I just wished she would come to me and tell me what she was feeling.

On the flip side of that, Lindsey showed her emotions as soon as she felt them. When she hit her terrible twos and she didn't get her way, she would throw herself on the floor. As she hit her head on the linoleum, she stopped crying and looked at me. I was so glad she was my third child because I just froze. I didn't want to comfort her and encourage that behavior, but I was worried she was hurt. We just looked at each other for a second and then she cried an I'm-in-pain cry. I waited for her to get up and then gave her a comforting hug and put some ice on her head. Whatever she was mad about was forgotten by both of us.

Later that day, Dan arrived home while the girls were playing outside. After a few minutes, Dan decided it was time for supper so he said, "It's time to go inside now."

I practically pushed him over as I ran to Lindsey just

as she was yelling, "No!" and started screaming. I put my hands under her head just in time as she threw herself onto the cement. I quickly laid her head on the cement and asked Dan to take the other two girls inside.

When Lindsey finished yelling, I said, "Let's go find Daddy." She jumped up and ran inside.

"When did that start?" Dan asked.

I explained what had happened earlier that day when she didn't get her way. It didn't take Lindsey long to learn that throwing herself on the floor didn't help her get her way . . . and it hurt. Soon, she would look at where she was and run to the carpet and *then* throw herself onto the floor. Dan and I would turn our heads to laugh at that move.

With Lindsey, you always knew where you stood. She would let her emotions out and wasn't afraid of saying what was on her mind. She didn't keep things inside, but would express them and move on. She would ask me for a hug if she needed one and tell me she didn't want one if I tried to hug her at the wrong time.

> *Accept your child's method to deal with their feelings, instead of trying to make them do it your way.*

Ashley always felt things intensely. She didn't cry, *she sobbed*. It was never easy to understand how much things were affecting her. Her emotions were always either on full blast or not at all. She had trouble telling us what she was feeling so she would write us notes. There was nothing worse than going to bed after a long day and hearing the crunch of paper under me. I could never just go to bed; I always had to turn on the light and read the heartfelt note. Of course, I couldn't do anything about it until morning. Ashley was sleeping peacefully because she had gotten rid of her bound-up feelings, but now *I* couldn't sleep. I had to figure out what was happening and get over my guilt that she couldn't talk to me.

The next day I would go to her and talk through the situation. I realized that Ashley didn't really want to talk to me. She preferred it if I wrote out my answer or response to her on paper, and she sometimes even gave me options to mark. But that is just not my style, so I struggled to adjust to her method. Once in a while I did, but most of the time I made her talk it out.

Integrity

Danielle was a sweet, caring girl, who when asked, couldn't lie. If she thought someone would get in trouble, she wouldn't tell, but I could tell she was lying. She had that half-grin on her face, just like her Dad did whenever he would try to keep a secret.

Ashley's world was entirely black and white, so if I asked her what happened, she would tell me. She didn't care if someone got in trouble; if I asked, she told. (The preschool teachers had to teach her not to tattle.) If she was the one to do it, she didn't want to get herself in trouble, but it was wrong to lie, so she didn't. She would find a clever way to try to avoid the answer or to look at the question in a unique way. For example, when I asked if she made her bed, she would say, "Yes."

When I would go to her room and see that her bed was not made she would explain, "You didn't ask if I made my bed today. I made it yesterday, so yes, I made my bed."

Ashley told the truth in her own black and white world, which sometimes was hard to figure out. When she was in sixth grade and was having trouble staying focused in her classes, she failed her hearing test at school so we took her to the doctor. She also failed *that* hearing test. So, naturally, she was sent to a specialist.

At that clinic, the test showed that she was trying to cheat, guessing the answer wrong. She believed she had a hearing problem. I asked her in front of the doctor, "Were you guessing when to raise your hand? Did you only raise it when you heard a noise?"

"Yes, I did it right," she cried.

I defended her in front of the doctor and said she was not a liar. With the test inconclusive, we left with no answers. She sat in the front of the classroom the rest of that year and no other issues were found. Years later, I found out she had lied. She thought she had a hearing problem, so she tried to prove it. In her black and white world, that was being honest.

> *Be ready to explain your child's uniqueness and justify their behavior.*

Lindsey could be an actress, which became obvious with her ability to lie. We called it *storytelling*. Her teachers helped us learn that label. At her kindergarten conference they asked if I was expecting another child. I explained I was not and felt a little fat. The teacher quickly explained that Lindsey was telling everyone that she was going to have a baby brother!

Another time, she came home from first grade and told me that her head hurt. She had fallen on the playground and hit her head. I was alarmed. She explained she went to the nurse twice because it hurt so much. I was furious she didn't have a note explaining this.

I looked at the clock. Of course it was after four and the school was closed. That night at the supper table, I was telling Dan about her fall and I got a thought.

"Lindsey, was the fall on the playground real or was it a story?"

"Oh, a story Mom!" Lindsey answered honestly. Thank goodness the school was closed when I first heard the story!

"Was this real or a story?" was a constant question Dan and I asked Lindsey. It even became a game between us, to see which one of us would forget to ask and be taken in by one of her *stories*. At one point, I realized it was time she outgrow the cute storytelling stage, so I sat down with Lindsey when she was in fourth grade and told her she had to learn to tell the truth. No more lying!

She looked up at me and said, "What if I just can't

learn how to tell the truth?"

That was hard to hear, that my little girl thought she couldn't stop lying. I told her, with tears in my eyes, that we would find a way together. Then I realized she just didn't know *how* to tell the truth! It didn't matter that she would get in trouble for lying. So I had to find a way to teach her *not* to lie, and after I tucked her into bed that night, I walked out of her room with tears running down my cheeks.

The answer came to me the next night as I was tucking her into bed. I had this habit of checking her toothbrush to see if it was wet. Then I would ask her if she brushed her teeth. This time I realized that I was asking her a question I already knew the answer to. I was setting her up to lie every night, but I wanted to set her up to succeed, so I went into my plan to help Lindsey learn to tell the truth.

"Lindsey, did you brush your teeth?"

"Yes," she replied.

Then I explained: "Now, Lindsey, we need to start telling the truth, but we are going to learn together. When you write with a pencil, what do you do when you make a mistake?"

"I erase it," Lindsey answered.

"So we are going to learn to erase our words. So let's erase that YES," I explained. I rubbed my lips with my fingers and made a funny noise. She laughed and did the same. I continued, "Okay, now you can correct your answer. So, have you brushed your teeth?"

"No," she replied as she scrambled happily out of

bed and to the bathroom to brush her teeth. After that, each time I wasn't sure if she was telling the truth, I would ask, "Do you need to erase that?"

It was a long process, but she would erase, laugh, and then tell the truth. I was so relieved I had found a fun way for her to learn to tell the truth.

Adapting to the Challenge

Just like with any job, I always seemed to be faced with a challenge; it just wasn't always the same child. Luckily, I read an article about labels for your children. If you label your child as shy, even if she demonstrates that behavior, she will continue to build that characteristic in the future. I did use them, but I tried to be aware of them and change them up. It seemed impossible not to label them. However, I had one label that did stick for Lindsey. She was just that kind of child, very active, full of mischief, and at times I would explain to others that with Lindsey, we had our *boy*, our *tom*boy. With three little girls, I was used to sand-covered clothes after a day at the park or after they played in the backyard sandbox. What I never expected was sand in their clothes coming *out* of the dryer. As I talked to some of the other moms, they said they had sand everywhere, too. Those moms had little boys. Finally, one day in the park I saw Lindsey putting sand in her pocket. I asked her what she was doing. She said, "Saving it for later."

That sounded like a little boy to me! It seemed to work out so much better if I would remind myself she was my boy (tomboy), because that was just how she behaved. She was just like me! My mom would smile whenever I talked to her about how I was struggling with Lindsey . . . it was a smile to confirm, "It's so great to see the pay back!"

Everything my friends complained about with their active boys I had in Lindsey. I watched Lindsey play basketball with a Little Tykes basketball hoop, but it was too boring for her, so she wore her rollerblades and played basketball because it was more exciting that way. Sometimes she would wear a rollerblade on one foot and use the skateboard with the other, because it was too simple to skateboard with just shoes on.

Lindsey was potty trained outside! She would be watching TV and then ask if she could go outside to play. She walked outside on the patio and wet her pants. (She did not pull them down, she just wet through everything.) Then she would try to just walk back into the house and sit back down to watch TV. I realized I was calmer when I walked outside, got the hose, and sprayed off the patio, than I was if I had to clean the pee up from the couch. But seriously, we *didn't have a boy,* just a tomboy! I quickly learned that when Lindsey asked to go outside to play while she was watching TV, she had

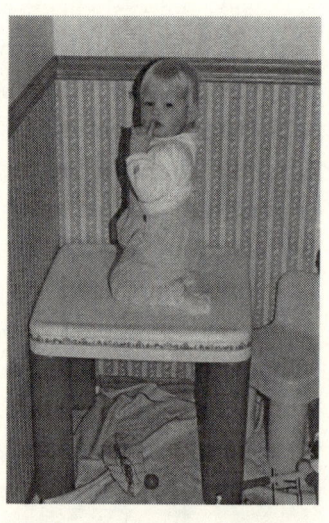

Lindsey caught climbing

to go to the bathroom. Of course she didn't end up going outside; she just went to the bathroom and came right back to the TV.

Potty training a younger child can lead to interesting conversation at the dinner table. One night, Dan was plain tired of the hearing about poop while eating, (I won't admit I was the one telling the story), so we decided there were *bathroom words*. If anyone used bathroom words at the table, they were excused to go to the bathroom to say those words. Danielle would go into the bathroom and start singing "Potty, potty, potty, poop, poop, poop."

When Ashley would use bathroom words at the table, I took her to the bathroom. Often when I did this, she'd cry and look at herself in the mirror. "I don't want to see me sad. I don't want to be in the bathroom."

"If you are done using bathroom words, then you can come back to the table," I told her.

"Oh, ok," she nodded and said, all done crying. This reinforced my understanding that her intense crying didn't mean she was feeling really hurt. She just dealt with everything intensely.

Lindsey had the best line at the table for bodily functions. She said, "My butt burped."

Dan and I were both laughing too much to say anything, but both nodded at each other when it happened. Yep, she was our boy (tomboy).

*Discipline is not always needed
to curb negative behavior.*

A Mommy's Road

❖ ❖ ❖

Until I was a parent, I didn't realize that we learned from observation. We watch the world around us and imitate what people do. That is how we learn to fit in to the world. Ashley didn't learn that way. Don't get me wrong; she is very intelligent and can learn anything from a book or have it verbally explained to her, but she doesn't learn from observation. Observation is how the other girls learned social interaction. Ashley just never got that. If we would read a book about it, she would get it. Thank God for the *Berenstain Bears*[4] books. They taught her a lot about fitting in to life as a toddler and a young child.

Ashley's birthday was just a month past the cutoff date for starting school, and with her high intelligence I knew she would be ready to start kindergarten one year early. When she was just three years old, I had her in three-year-old preschool class three days a week and in a four-year-old class two days a week. I was trying to determine which age group she would fit best, as she would either be the oldest or the youngest. She mothered the younger kids in her 'correct' age group, and our big concern was her being bored and not challenged in school.

Ashley 'reading' my *Raising Your Spirited Child*[5]

I even asked her doctor what he thought of starting her in school a year earlier. He pointed out she was in the 90% for her height so she wouldn't be the shortest. He did point out to think about her being the youngest to get her driver's license and would be dating older boys: in other words, look all the way through her life as you make this decision. As it turned out, the school district's birth date rule was firm, there was NO WAY we could start her in kindergarten early! So she waited to start school when she was five years old and 11 months. I pushed to have her tested at the start of the year. She only got two questions wrong on the **end of the year** test and was moved into first grade after just two weeks of kindergarten. Dan and I had thoroughly thought through this decision, and we felt it was then right decision for Ashley. She would have a lot of challenges emotionally, but at least she shouldn't be as bored in the classroom.

Ashley doesn't transition well, so doing two transitions in such a short time was a challenge. She would get off the bus and by the time she got to the front door of our house, she was bawling. Of course, at first I thought something happened at school. I gave her hugs and asked tons of questions. Nothing bad had happened. All she would say was, "I missed you too much," and then sob some more.

After checking with her teacher, I found out she was perfectly fine at school and she didn't seem homesick at all. She saved all of the drama for me. After several days of this, I decided I had to change this behavior. Of course I had already taught her that you get tons of attention if you sob when you come home, so I knew it was going to take a while to get her to change her behavior. Ashley never forgets.

I decided we would role play. When she arrived home, I said, "Ashley that's not how you come home from school. Let's play a game. I will be Ashley coming home from school and you pretend to be Mommy waiting for Ashley."

I went outside the house, closed the door, and left Ashley standing in the entry way of the house. I then opened the door and said to Ashley, "Mommy, I am so happy to see you. I had a great day at school." I reached down and gave her a really big hug.

I encouraged her to think about what Mommy would say.

She replied, "What did you do at school?"

Then I made her go outside the door and *be* Ashley coming home again and I would *be* Mommy. She, of course, would giggle at this silly game. And the very next day, she came home in tears!

I leaned down and said to her, "We don't come home that way. You'll be Mommy, I'll be Ashley."

Again, we role played and then switched back, and Ashley had to come through the door again. We had to do this quite a few times. There were days she would remember the first time, and then there were days she would be in tears again. But over time, she did not need the role-playing game.

> *Try to see that your child is not 'challenging;' consider that each child has traits that are challenging to you.*

My Role as a Manager

✧ ✧ ✧

I was sometimes the challenging child. Even though I was the parent, I still had things to learn (when do we not?). Once, from a distance, I observed Danielle playing with several stuffed animals. She had them all lined up and said to them, "Just a minute, Mommy will be right there."

I thought, *oh so cute, she is imitating me.* She continued to play for a couple of minutes. Then I heard her say, "Just a minute. I know it seems like Mommy is taking forever but that's Mommy's minute!"

Ouch, that one hurt. I realized I was too busy for Danielle too often. She had definitely gotten the idea that Mom's minute could last forever. It was time for me to turn my focus back on my children and off my task at hand.

I know I was supposed to be the adult, but sometimes I found myself not acting like one. At first I thought the girls always got into more trouble whenever I had a lot to do. If I was getting ready for out-of-town relatives to stay for a few days, the girls always seemed to argue. I would try to clean, they would fight. I would try to cook, they would take the shortest nap in history. I just wanted to get things done, but they wanted to help. Of course I would snap at them, yell at them to behave, and tell them they could help next time . . . but nothing seemed to work. It wasn't until I would just give up and sit down with them, did things start to go better. The more I wanted to get done, the more I ignored them, which never worked. If I remembered to focus on them and then do a task, and switch back and forth, I did actually accomplish some things . . . But I would never remember that. This seemed to be something I needed to continue to learn.

One day I caught myself yelling at the girls: "STOP YELLING!"

Nothing happened, so I yelled louder. Then all of a sudden I actually heard what I was saying. I stopped, walked up stairs to the girls and gathered them around me. I told them, "Mommy has made a big mistake. Mommy has been yelling. I think I need to learn to stop yelling. Do you think I should be punished for yelling?"

"I think you should say you are sorry," Danielle said.

"I think you should stop yelling," Lindsey shared.

Ashley look confused and said, "Mommy can't be punished."

I told each girl I was sorry for yelling at them all of the time. I gave each of them a hug as I apologized. Then I explained that I would try hard to come to them and look at them when I was talking, instead of just yelling up the stairs. They all agreed that would be nice. I pointed out that if Mommy does something wrong, she should be punished, or given a time-out, just like the girls had to do sometimes. That's when a light bulb came on. I *did* need a time-out! I was yelling sometimes because I was being too lazy to go to the girls. But most of the time I was yelling because I was out of patience. I needed to take a breath. My yelling wasn't solving the problem. I told the girls that when Mommy yells, she would need to have a time-out.

"Where are you going to have your time-out?"

Ashley wanted to know.

"I will go to my bedroom all by myself for my time-out," I said. "Since I was yelling, I will go have a time out right now." I walked downstairs and set the kitchen timer for five minutes, walked into my bedroom and laid on my bed. Of course, the girls walked in one minute later.

I looked at them calmly and said, "I have to be alone until the timer goes off for my time-out." So they all ran off and waited. As soon as the timer went off, they came running back. We all gathered on my bed and I once again apologized for yelling.

"That's okay," they all said at once.

It was a silly game, perhaps, but it was a lesson I needed to remember. When I was feeling like a discontent child, I needed to walk away, take a breath, and become Mommy again. I wish I could say I stopped yelling, but it was a constant work in progress.

> *In the heat of the moment, you are not your best. If it is safe, walk away, breathe, and come back with a new perspective.*

Equal but Different

I never thought I would treat my children differently. However, that was the only way to treat them, as they were all three very totally unique children. Danielle, as a toddler, would cry whenever her dad would say 'no' to her about something. He had to learn how to talk softly and say 'no' with a gentler voice. She would test her boundaries consistently to see if the rules had changed, but she didn't need to be yelled at. Just a gentle reminder was all she ever needed. In that same vein, it was easy to put Danielle into time-outs. I would simply remove her from the situation, put her on a chair, and tell her to wait. I then walked away and timed a minute in my head. She had no problem staying in her chair and waiting like she was told. Sometimes she didn't even cry, and it worked. When I tried that same thing with Ashley, she would scream and cry. Also, to compound both of our frustration, Danielle was there to entertain her and talk to her, which thoroughly distracted from the discipline. So, in order to give Ashley a time-out, I had to carry her to the steps to isolate her from Danielle. Now Danielle couldn't see her, so Danielle would keep asking, "All done?"

"No," I would yell, but then I got distracted with how long Ashley was there, so I set a minute timer for one minute for Ashley and two minutes for Danielle (one minute per age of child). That way I could ignore the constant questions, *'time up?'* or *'all done'* from both the girls. It also made the timer the enemy instead of me. I would just remind both of them to wait for the beep.

When Lindsey was old enough to get into things, I put her on the step as I did with Ashley, but because of her personality, instead of staying put, she would just see how far up she could climb before I noticed. Or, she would disappear around the corner. So I got mad, grabbed her, snatched a chair and put her in it right in front of the timer. I reset the timer and watched her so she wouldn't get down. As she got more verbal, she started to explain her behavior, question how much time she had left, etc. Of course, I got sucked in to her conversations. I would get so mad. Finally, I realized I had to zip my mouth. I would just point to the timer and wait. At last, she would just sit in the chair and watch the timer go down.

It ended up to be a blessing that they all had their time-outs in different locations. Now when more than one of them needed a time-out, I could put them into their correct location for their time-out. I would then split the difference between their ages for the length of the time-out.

Ashley never tested the boundaries and the rules just to see if they had changed. She always followed the rules and would never forget any lesson she learned. When Ashley became mobile, I showed her what would happen if she went too close to the top of the stairs. I pushed her dolly (aptly named Dollie) down the stairs and said, "That could happen to you if play on the stairs."

She cried and I felt bad, so I gave Dollie a hug. Thankfully it taught her the lesson, and Ashley didn't want to fall tumbling down the stairs like her dolly, so she would crawl by the stairs and wait until I would come help her. Yes, that may have been mean, but I was tired of helping her older sister over the gates and climbing them myself. When Ashley was old enough, I taught her how to climb up and down the stairs herself and explained it was safe for her to do the steps alone. She was bigger now and could do it better than Dollie.

Lindsey pushed the boundaries like Danielle, but to have Lindsey even hear us we *had* to yell. It was hard for me to get Lindsey's attention. She was the one girl I spanked because she would keep doing things I told her not to. At least that worked, but in a few days I saw her hit her sister and I found myself saying, "Don't hit!"

I realized I had taught her to do that, so I had to find a new way. Later that day, we were outside playing and Lindsey took a step into the street. I yelled, ran, grabbed her quickly, was about to spank her, but stopped. I then explained to her, "If you go into the street and a car comes," just as a car drove by, "you will get hit." And I clapped my hands together loudly.

"I don't want to get hit," she cried.

The next time we were outside, she started running toward the street, I looked up and down our street and seeing no cars, I watched, anticipating she would run into the street again . . . but she didn't. She stopped. I ran up to her and gave her a big hug. From that moment on, she would run as fast as she could to the curb and then stop. Each and every time I checked for cars, and every time she stopped. Then one time there was a car coming, and my heart stopped. The driver of the car quickly slammed on her brakes, but Lindsey stopped right at the curb. The driver shook her head and drove on. It wasn't the best answer, but I finally knew she got it. I had to make Lindsey cry so that I knew she heard me and wouldn't just ignore me.

Knowing that the girls all reacted differently to any

situation was a great thing, if only I could remember that on a daily basis. Many times I would have Danielle in tears over the simplest thing because I forgot that it was Danielle I was talking to, and not Lindsey. One afternoon, I had just left Lindsey's room at naptime after telling her not to sit on the window sill because it was dangerous. As I reached the bottom step, I remembered it was Lindsey I was talking to, not Ashley, who would follow a rule. I quietly walked back up the stairs and pushed open the door just a crack. Lindsey was sitting nicely on the windowsill, looking down from the second story with only a screen keeping her in! I carefully snuck up behind her and gently pushed her toward the screen (while grabbing her shoulders tightly) as I asked, "What are you doing?"

She jumped as she was surprised, and explained that she was just looking out the window. I went on to describe what could happen if she slipped and fell through the screen to the ground below.

She looked down, with me holding on to her tightly, and said, "I would bounce on that thing."

She thought the top of the air conditioner looked like a giant spring she could bounce off of. I quickly realized Super Human Lindsey thought she would not get hurt falling from a second story window.

I explained that if she fell, she would end up hurt, behind the fence in the side yard of our house. She would be hidden behind the locked gate by the big bushes and couldn't get out. I wouldn't know where she was, she would be lost and hurt, and be stuck back there. She then got scared and started to cry. She didn't want to be lost. I explained that she wouldn't be lost as long as she didn't sit on the windowsill ever again. She nodded with tears in her eyes, promising she wouldn't. Thank goodness I remembered that it was Lindsey that I was dealing with and I had gone back up those stairs.

In the Rearview Mirror of My Role as a Manager

Looking back, I was worried that having three girls so close in age left them with little individual attention. So at the end of each day, I would give them that special one-to-one moment and tuck them into bed. Even when they were certainly old enough to go to bed on their own, I would still tuck them in. That was my individual time with them each and every day. It was a time they could tell me something they didn't want to say in front of their sisters, and it helped us to end our day on a positive note and with a reminder of the love we shared.

Just like at a job where I would be constantly juggling multiple things, as a mom, I was constantly dealing with unique girls. I would start to treat them all alike and I would be prompted that it didn't work. Danielle would be in tears because her feelings were hurt, Lindsey would just go do it again because she never got the message, while Ashley would ask why. Sometimes I just had to keep relearning the same lesson, over and over again.

The advantage of having three unique girls was that it was easy not to compare one to the other. I treated them differently because that is just how they acted. They had different interests and excelled at different things. The challenge was just remembering which one I was dealing at that time. However, the girls would compare themselves to one another. They would either brag to their sister or point out their own failures. I would just remind them how they were different people and that was not something they could change. It was not a failure to be different from one another; it was just the way it was. The important thing was that they didn't compare themselves to one another; their responsibility was to do the best THEY could do.

As a mom, I never wanted to treat them differently. If you had asked me before I had children if I would treat them differently I would have said, 'Of course not!' But with three unique girls, it became impossible to treat them the same. So I worked on hiding the difference from them until I started hearing, "You love her more!"

To that, I would simply say, "I love you all equally, but I never said I would treat you the same. I will always treat you differently. It will be equal, but different."

Ashley and Danielle helping Lindsey

"That's not fair," would be the complaint back from one of them, inevitably.

"Life's not fair; get used to it," was my answer.

Chapter 7:
Project Testing

Being able to stay home with my children was such a blessing, but I quickly learned I was a much better mom out in public. The days I stayed home, I had less patience and was sucked into their sibling conflicts. All of the little things they did seemed to bug me. When I was out in public, I had more patience and I was better able to ignore those little things. I was more distracted from their little battles and could focus more on their positive behavior.

Trial and Error: Being in Public

Whenever we went grocery shopping, it had to be well planned. I had a completed grocery list and packed a snack and a juice for each girl. We would head out after naps with everyone well rested and hopefully in good moods. I put two kids into one cart, sitting inside facing each other and Lindsey sat in the cart facing away from her sisters, while I pulled a second cart for food. The girls learned to sit nicely like that until aisle #5 where they would get their snacks. Then in aisle #7 they would get their juice boxes. (The first numbers they could identify as they got older were 5 and 7.) As we would get towards the end of the store, the food cart would be getting full, so Danielle would get out and help push the kid cart so I could start to add groceries to that cart, too. As she sat in the cart, Ashley would get buried beneath groceries (which she loved); it was like being at the beach and getting buried with sand. Then Dan would meet us at the store after he got off work, to help pack up the groceries and haul them to the car. This was before cell phones, so it had to be planned ahead of time. He would just come to the store and look for us, and hopefully we would be almost done. We were able to get through the check-out without much struggle because they were happy to see Daddy and were distracted from the temptations at the checkout.

Now, don't get me wrong, it wasn't always this smooth. Because of Ashley, I learned to never give in, not even once, since once she was taught a rule, she always followed it. This worked in her favor, too. Whenever I gave in to her, to her, that meant I always would. So . . . my girls never got a treat at the checkout counter, because one treat meant three treats, and they had already had their treats in aisles #5 and #7. If they ever did get a treat, it was put into the grocery cart and taken home to be eaten there.

> *Be consistent. Kids don't understand why one day it's ok to get a treat and another day it isn't.*

There was a time when I was heading into the grocery store to pick up a few things with just Lindsey and she decided to have a temper tantrum. She just wouldn't listen to reason, so I decided it was best to just leave. I left my cart in the middle of some aisle and carried my screaming kid out of the store. As I was driving home with her still screaming in her car seat, I wondered if anyone thought I was stealing a child. Then I realized that no one in their right mind would steal a kid who was screaming at the top of her lungs!

◆ ◆ ◆

On rainy days or in the winter, we would go to the mall just to walk around and window shop, and that's when I taught the girls say *'goodbye'* to everything. It was the best way for them to move from one place to the next without a temper tantrum. I received many strange looks as my girls would hug a pillow or wave at the pet store window and say, "Goodbye, see you next time," but it worked.

Being out in public, things didn't always go as planned (as every parent can understand). When the girls were not able to behave, I had them apologize to random people. They had to apologize to more random people than I can remember. They even said they were sorry to the store clerks for picking up an object that I had told them not to touch. One day I was buying a few things, and Danielle wanted one of those impulse-buys at the check-out counter.

"No," I said, my voice stern.

She started to whine, so I added, "Absolutely not, now that you are whining for it."

Later that afternoon, when I took Lindsey out to

hold her, I found that very same item in the stroller. Miraculously, Danielle had no idea how it got there.

"It must have fell into the stroller, Mommy."

She had her classic look of dishonesty on her face. after I had a few minutes to think, we went back to that store. I found the very same sales clerk who heard me tell her she couldn't have it. I had Danielle give it back to her and tell her we had not paid for it. The sales clerk wisely, yet sternly, reminded her to never do that again.

> *Remember you are teaching your child responsibility–or the lack of it–at a very early age.*

Sometimes *I* had to be the good example. I remember once something fell off the shelf and broke when we were near it. I didn't see any of the girls bump it, but I knew if I walked away I would be teaching them *not* to be responsible. It was a tough choice because it was an expensive item and I really thought we were going to have to pay for it. I took the item to the counter and accepted responsibility. The clerk also used this as an excellent teaching opportunity. She looked at me and the girls and said, "That's okay . . . accidents do happen. Just don't let it happen again."

As an adult, I understand that accidents happen, but that was a hard lesson for Ashley, in particular, to learn. A few years later, we were in a restaurant and the waitress spilled a cold drink off her tray onto Ashley. Knowing Ashley's reaction would be intense, I swiftly grabbed her, asked for the car keys from Dan, and carried her out of the restaurant. We happened to be on vacation so we had suitcases in our car outside. I sat her in the backseat, pulled off her cold, soaked top, and told her to take off her shorts as I dug through the suitcase for a dry outfit. Within a minute, she had changed clothes and I had a dry shirt on since my shirt had gotten wet as I carried her out of the restaurant. We walked back to our table just as Dan and our waitress had finished cleaning up the mess.

The waitress was visibly upset and apologized for what had happened. I turned to her. "It's okay, it was an accident." Then I turned to Ashley and said, "It was an accident, right?"

Ashley nodded, but after the waitress left, she shared her confusion. "Mommy, why is it okay that she spilled cold pop all over me? You said it was okay."

I tried to explain it to Ashley. "It wasn't okay that she spilled on you. I said it was an accident. Accidents happen. No one wants them to happen, but sometimes they do. Tonight it happened to you and you got all wet. Sometimes we spill and the waitress has to clean it up. It just happens. We just have to learn to accept they are sorry if they caused us pain, but we don't need to be mad at them. We don't want others to be mad at us if we are the cause of the accident the next time."

She was still upset about it, but was content enough to finish eating. When the bill came, Dan told Ashley her meal was free because she had gotten all wet. She was glad the waitress had to pay for her mistake. She just couldn't understand the concept of accidents.

Behavior in a restaurant seemed like a hard thing to

learn. I realized at fast food restaurants and at home, the food was there when the girls sat down. The whole idea of learning to wait to get the food was a new concept, so the first thing was to figure out how to keep them content while we waited. Many restaurants have crayons and coloring menus for children, which worked for a while, but as soon as the girls would order, they thought they should have the food NOW! Still . . . they had to wait. So we let them eat ice cubes with a spoon. (Do you know how long a child can be entertained with a spoon and ice cubes?) They also learned to be careful or they got a wet lap, but at least it was just water. Cold water, but just water!

> *Be willing to take your child to a restaurant so they will learn manners and patience.*

As they got older, they did better, but just when I thought they were old enough to behave, they would prove me wrong. One time when we were eating at an outdoor table at a restaurant, I didn't think about how eating outdoors would be different than indoors, but it was to them. They couldn't understand the concept that we were at a restaurant, and no matter what I did, they would not behave.

When we were finished eating, I had them go over to the next table and apologize to two guys who had been giving us the evil eye the whole time. They didn't seem too happy to be interrupted again with the apology, but I was teaching my girls a lesson. The girls were embarrassed because I had them go to the next table to apologize to those customers, too. I usually tried to evaluate who would understand, and I was the happiest when they didn't say, "That's okay."

I would wink at those who would say, "You won't do that again, will you?"

The most dramatic restaurant scene was on Mother's Day. We were waiting in line to be seated at a very busy restaurant. The girls were elementary school age, but waiting in line was still a challenge. There were a couple of seats, but not enough for all of them. Dan tried to teach the girls to be nice to me on Mother's Day and told them, "Let Mom have one of the seats."

The three of them pushed and argued about who got to sit next to me as we waited. Finally, I said, "ENOUGH!" (Sometimes I did over react.)

I stood up and walked out the door in silence. As we went back to the car, they cried because we weren't eating at the restaurant. Dan reminded them it was Mother's Day and they ruined it for me. I went to our bedroom at home and let Dan deal with three sad kids and a mad wife . . . not an easy day to be a dad. We ended up going out for supper that night and they were perfect angels at the restaurant. (I learned to look at the day before Mother's Day or my birthday as a gift of personal time. Dan would take all of the girls out shopping for my gift. I had the gift of time for myself; often this time was better than the gift I opened the next day.)

Collaboration

There were many times I needed to rely on others moms

for additional support. At first that support was from a small group of moms I met with each week at playgroup. I was able to watch them not only interact with their own children, but also with my girls. It was an easy transition to start leaving Danielle with one of them so I could go to an appointment, and it didn't take long before we traded babysitting. By the time we all had two children, we noticed that it wasn't difficult to add another child or two into our homes, so Nancy and I started to take turns watching our four kids one morning a week. That gave me two mornings off a week.

After I had Lindsey, I didn't like to leave three children when they only left two, so I encouraged the use of tickets. We paid one ticket per hour per child. That way, I would watch their two children for three hours and get 'paid' six tickets. When I would leave my three girls for two hours and I would get 'paid' six tickets back. I believed that was a fair practice. It was a blessing to have the support of these other moms.

Then we moved to Arizona and we left those closely trusted families behind. Out of desperation, I had to trust one mom, Becky, in our new place right away. It worked out very well for her to watch the three girls. She started to leave her son with me a few times for her appointments, but I had three girls and she had just one son, so I pushed for a ticket system, and talked about the babysitting co-op I had with the other group of moms before we moved. She loved that idea and thought it would be a great addition to our playgroup. We shared this idea with the other moms. Everyone loved the idea of being able to have a doctor or dentist appointment without having our husbands take time off work to watch our children, or have to bring our children to our appointments. We saw the added benefit of getting to know these moms and families better and building trusting relationships.

That's how The Children Christian Cooperative, a babysitting co-op, was started. We included the word Christian since the playgroup started as a group from our church, even though other moms now attended the playgroup; we liked the idea that it was still Christian families. We made a directory with parent names, children names, ages, addresses, and phone numbers (it was before emails and cell phones). We included a description for each family that answered questions that we wanted to know about the family and their house, but we may be too embarrassed to ask. So the directory listed: was there was a pool, and if so, was it fenced? Were there guns in the home, and if so, were they hidden and locked? Did anyone smoke, and if so, in the house? Did they have a pet, and if so, what type of pet?

Each family was given one pack of tickets for each child they had. With the limited number of tickets, families would have to reciprocate babysitting or they would run out, so we figured there wouldn't be a way for someone to take advantage of others. A pack of tickets included: 20 pink one-hour tickets, 10 blue half-hour tickets, and one yellow overnight ticket. At the time, most of us didn't think we would ever leave our child overnight, but one of the husbands thought that would be a good idea so we had the option to use it in the future. The cost of babysitting was one ticket per child per hour. There was an added option to pay more tickets if you wanted to have your child babysat in your own home.

Each family would decide who they wanted to watch. There were no requirements or suggestions on who babysat; this was just a list of options. Most moms had already established relationships within the group and some families already knew each other well. It was suggested that people have play dates for the children, that way the moms would get to know each other better, see how well the children got along, and see the layout of the home before using them as babysitters. We scheduled a couple of kick-off family events to help everyone get to know each other.

> *A babysitting co-op is a modern day extended family. If you don't have a large extended family to rely on, create your own.*

The Christian Children Co-op grew with additional families and as people had babies. I loved the idea of the tickets because as I would leave my three girls with someone with one child, I knew it was more work than when they left their one child with me. I was able to pay them more tickets, one ticket, per child, per hour. I loved it and so did the other families. Many of us started having date nights again with our spouses and the kids loved having friends over. Dan was surprised that it was a fun family night to have additional children in to play with our girls. It wasn't a chore. The family relationship grew to the point that many of us did use the overnight coupons and Dan and I were able to get away for a night without waiting for grandparents to visit. It truly was a win-win.

There were times, however, when we needed more than just The Christian Children Cooperative. The time Lindsey was really sick with the flu and I had taken her to Urgent Care, Dan was home with the other two girls and had even put them to bed before I called to say I was taking Lindsey to the hospital. He really wanted to see Lindsey and support me, but he wasn't going to wake up the older two. It was 10:00 p.m., so he didn't feel comfortable calling someone in the co-op to drive over and watch the girls. I told him to call Toni, our neighbor, and the mother of our babysitter. He did, and even though she was already in bed, her husband George said he would do it.

Since the girls were sleeping, George came over and sat in our living room while Dan drove to the hospital to see Lindsey and comfort me. Dan only stayed away for a couple of hours and headed back home and the girls never woke up.

It wasn't until a year later, after we got to know both George and Toni better, did we hear the other side of the story. George was sitting in our living room when he realized that Danielle and Ashley didn't know him. They knew Toni and Allison, his wife and daughter, but they really didn't know him that well yet. He told us he started to freak out, wondering if they would wake up and see him and flip out that this strange man was in their house and both their parents were gone. But they never woke up and he never said anything until months later.

Lindsey ended up in the hospital for five days, and Dan couldn't take every day off to be with the other two girls . . . and I wasn't going to leave Lindsey. I had Dan pull out The Christian Children Cooperative directory and call someone in the group. I wasn't thinking straight because I didn't tell him who I had already used before, so he just called the first name on the list. This young mom of nine-month-old twins and an almost three year old came to our house to watch Danielle and Ashley for most of a day. I trusted her, but never would have asked her because she already had three kids. However, she was more than willing to do it and did a great job. I will never forget how happy I was to have an established directory of trusted individuals that my husband and I could reach out to in our time of need. I was able to be with Lindsey 24/7 physically and emotionally because of the other moms in our Christian Children Cooperative.

> *Be willing to help other parents, as there will be times you will need help in return.*

Report to the Boss

I knew I had to teach the girls about stranger danger, but I never liked the idea. With super sensitive Ashley, all I had to do was to start a conversation and she would be

Project Testing

in tears. Then Super Human Lindsey thought she could outrun any stranger, or beat him up. She was never afraid. Danielle just loved everyone, so why wouldn't you help someone find a puppy? How could I teach them to be safe? I felt that to keep them safe I had to either scare them (which was already the case with Ashley) or change their given personalities.

One day, not long after I told them to not talk to strangers, just as we were leaving the grocery store, the girls asked me if I "knew those people."

"What people?" I asked.

"The people in the grocery store," Danielle explained. "You were talking to strangers."

Now I was completely torn. If I continued on the scare-tactic strategy, I would have socially closed off, rude individuals for children. Luckily I had read about a new idea on how to keep your children safe. The concept was that you taught them to ask or report to you, the parent. I loved it.

So from that, I taught my kids to always tell me where they were going. At the playground, they had to come to me to tell me which play area they were going to be at in the park. In other words, I could always look up and see Ashley at the slide, Danielle at the swing, and Lindsey at the monkey bars. I knew where they would be the minute I looked up. When Danielle left the swing, she would run back to tell me she was heading over to the monkey bars to play with Lindsey. "Okay," I would say.

With three kids, I had to be able to look up and count to three within a second or my heart would stop, so it was really easy for me to enforce. Also, kids have tons of energy, so for them to run all the way over to me to report their next adventure was just great fun. They never said, "I have to run all the way over here to tell you that?"

I would trick them into doing it, too. Sometimes when it was time to head home, I would wait until someone would forget to tell me where they were. I would yell one girl's name and she would come running. I told her I had lost her and I thought she was on the swing. I would yell to the other two that we had to leave NOW, because someone didn't tell me where they were. And we would go home. They learned.

Other times, I would hide on them to teach them how it felt to be lost. So when they were all playing in the park, I would move. They would come back to find me and then start crying. I would say, "Oh, I am sorry I moved. How did it feel not to know where I was? That is how I feel if I don't know where you are. That is why you always tell me where you are, so we never have to be sad or scared."

They quickly agreed. Our stranger-danger rule was based on keeping each other informed. They were taught that if someone asks them to do something for them, just run back to Mom so she knows where you are. I wasn't asking them to make any new decisions; they were always keeping me informed. I just hoped if Danielle was asked by a stranger to help find their puppy, she would run to me to tell me she was helping find a puppy. I truly didn't trust that she would, but I hoped she would. I also knew I didn't want to scare her to never trust anyone, so I believed it was the best I could do and prayed for her safety.

Another great example of this happened with Dan. We hadn't been in Arizona long and he had a man come out to talk to him about our pool. We had never had a pool so he needed to learn how to care for it. I was gone, the girls were watching TV, and he told them he would be out back with the pool guy. He was back there longer than he thought he would be, and of course the girls were watching TV and didn't hear where he would be. Soon, Dan heard screaming and crying. He went into the house to see the three girls hugging each other and crying. They thought their dad had left them! Dan's heart was broken at the sight of all of them hugging and crying. He joined their hugs and cried with them. He explained to them where he was and that he had told them, but they just kept crying that he had left them. (Dan doesn't know what happened to the pool guy; he must have just left in the middle of this scene.)

When I returned later that afternoon, Dan told me what had happened. When I asked the girls about it, Danielle said, "Dad just disappeared."

"He didn't even tell us, like you're supposed to," Ashley stated.

"He was gone a long time," Lindsey accused.

"I told you," Dan explained. "But you were watching TV when I told you. I am sorry I was out back longer than I thought I would be, but I thought you knew where I was."

I took the opportunity to point out to the girls that was why we had the rule of telling Mommy or Daddy where they were all of the time. "I guess we also need to be sure the person is listening when we tell them." (I also noticed Danielle and Ashley hadn't heard what Dan said. Lindsey did, but it was longer than she thought.) I explained to Dan that he had to stand in front of the TV or turn it off when he was talking to the kids! (He didn't know I had been doing that to him for years.) It was a great lesson for the girls to be on the receiving end of, as they never questioned the rule for years to come.

❖ ❖ ❖

As the girls got older, I had to teach more scary lessons, which never went easily when all three girls were in the same room. The girls were walking just two blocks home from the bus stop in our *'safe'* neighborhood and one day, a child went missing in a city nearby on their way home from school. It was time to remind them to report to me. I gathered the girls together to talk about the dangerous world. I asked what would they do if someone in a white van offered them a ride? (Why do I always say a white van?) Ashley started to cry because she was scared. Danielle thought that was nice of them to stop and ask. Lindsey thought that was kind of silly and she would run home. I continued the discussion. Finally, Ashley asked the black and white question, "What if the van is black?"

I pointed out it didn't matter what color the van was . . . just don't get rides from other people, ever!

Then Danielle asked, "What if someone we know wants to give us a ride home?"

At first, I almost said they could ride with family friends, and then I remembered that most abductions were from people the family knew. I decided if I had a friend pick them up, I could give them a secret word so the girls would know it was safe, so we created safe words for each child. They learned not take a ride from someone, even a friend, unless they knew the safe words. They loved having safe words; it felt special.

One time we actually had to use our safe words. Lindsey and I were in the middle of getting her finger stitched at Urgent Care when it was time for the girls to get home from school. I had my friend, Sandy, pick them up at the bus stop and take them home. I knew they would just go with Sandy, since they knew her well. But at the last second I remembered the safe words and told Sandy to say, "Honey bear and pumpkin pie, your mom told me to pick you up."

Sandy didn't understand, but the girls did. They were so excited to tell me that Sandy had used the safe words when she picked them up. They even told their dad about the safe words at supper that night. It wasn't until then that I believed they wouldn't go without the safe words, even though I worried that Lindsey would trust anyone she knew; there was no way to teach her fear.

The world continued to creep into our lives and into our deep discussions with the shooting at Columbine High School. Once again, I gathered the girls around the table, Danielle in third grade, Ashley in second, and

Lindsey in kindergarten. Ashley cried the whole time. I started by just asking them what they would do if they found themselves in a situation like this, but I quickly saw that their safety was very much out of my control. The only thing I could tell them was to lay still and pray. I realized that all we had was our faith that God would keep us safe.

The Value of Education
The biggest overall influence on the girls, besides their family, was school and their teachers. Their teachers taught them everything from waiting in-line, manners, respect, asking questions, not tattling, cooperation, and working together, all while teaching them facts. I have total respect for the teaching profession and have a world of gratitude to the teachers in my girls' lives.

Supporting teachers was easy for me to do because I was a teacher and I was taught to trust and respect them. That doesn't mean I didn't question them or challenge their behaviors, but in front of others, especially the girls, I always supported them.

Dan had the opposite reaction. He didn't respect teachers and always challenged them. Even though he was taught to respect them, his personal experience with some of his teachers had taught him differently. When he knew something to be true and had challenged his teachers, they had not reacted well. His experience taught him to doubt what knowledge teachers truly had. I believed it was important to teach our girls to respect their teachers, and if there was a need to question their knowledge, they needed to do it with respect. I had to constantly tell Dan to be quiet in front of the girls. I didn't always succeed, so I am sure the girls got a mixed message from us.

Danielle loved kindergarten, but it was exhausting for her. She went in the morning and rode the bus home at lunchtime. In the afternoon, she would take a two-hour nap. As I heard other parents struggle with their cranky kindergarteners in the afternoon, I realized a kindergartener taking a nap was unusual, but it was exactly what Danielle needed and it worked for our family schedule. I just didn't tell the other moms about it, because I felt it was wrong. It wasn't until years later that I figured out that Danielle just needed time alone more than she needed a nap. She is an introvert, so all that time with other kids exhausted her. She gets her energy from being alone. She used her nap time to recharge in more ways than just sleep.

That year was the end of naps. As she adjusted to being in school all day, it seemed to go well. When she returned home at the end of the day, she would tell me all about her day during snack time and then she was ready for time to herself. The one thing I discovered about her school was they put the reading and extras in the morning and the math in the afternoon, but Danielle was not her best after lunch. I even tried to convince the schools that they should switch up the schedules for kids. Some of the students wouldn't be their best in the morning and over time would get behind in reading, just like Danielle was getting behind in math. By the time

Danielle was in third grade, she should have known all of her multiplication tables. She didn't. So she had a tutor throughout the summer. She was able to learn it quickly and started the next year all caught up. She told me much later she thought she was dumb in math because she had a tutor. Where did she get that label?

> *Labels will sneak into our lives; listen for them.*

When the girls were in early elementary school, I was able to help out in the classrooms. I would do anything from staple papers together, make copies, listen to the students in the girls' classroom read out loud, and chaperone field trips. When the girls were young, they loved me being in their classrooms and going to lunch with them in the cafeteria. I, too, loved to see them in their school environment. It was great to observe them interact with their friends. As the girls got older, it was less acceptable for me to help out in the classrooms and if I tried, I would often get tasks to do in a work room, which is not what I wanted to do. The girls were now in later elementary school and didn't like to see me at their school; it was like I was invading their space. However, parents were always needed on their field trips. I realized it was important for Dan to see them in this environment, too, so I encouraged him to attend some of the field trips with the girls. The girls felt super special when Dad took time off work to go on their field trip with them.

The girls participated in many school programs. It was their chance to be on stage and show off what they had learned. It started in preschool with a holiday and an end-of-year program. As a parent, I looked at that group of children, and found my little one who was the cutest, most

First day with all 3 girls in school!

talented one up there. Of course everyone felt that way, as all of the parents were bursting with pride. In elementary school, there would be one program a year to show us parents what our children had learned in music class and many times, incorporate information they had discovered in history. I was always amazed at the talent of the music teachers and the skill it took for them to orchestrate the whole program. To be able to have over 125 students on stage, standing right next to each other, not only cooperating, but performing, was so incredible. I believed through these events, the girls gained poise and self-confidence just by being in front of others. My hope was they would keep that confidence throughout life as they had to stand up for themselves. I was entertained by the different personalities I would see on stage: from the shy ones who stood very still and barely moved their lips, to the animated ones who were the drama queens. But each and every child received the applause of a job well done at the end of each song and would receive a standing ovation at the end of the program. Now the students were bursting with pride in themselves.

As I attended at least three of these events a year, I witnessed the same scene each and every time. As the children took their place in the front of the audience, each of them began to scan the audience, searching for their special person or two. I could see their faces change from a nervous panic to a look of relief, or even a smile as they found *that* person. When they saw that person in the audience, the child felt their love and support. To that child, at that moment, they knew someone in the audience was there to see them. I would watch their faces shine when they saw that one person in the audience, or the fear and sadness that continued on their faces when they couldn't locate that person. I would sense those feelings grow as they began to feel like they were on that stage all alone, even though they were standing with their whole class. Other parents witnessed the same thing as they watched the children on the stage. Some parents even stepped out of their own comfort zone to wave and yell at their child so they would know they were there. In the moment the child spots their parents, they were reassured and relieved that they were loved and supported. They were the center of attention for that person in that moment.

As I watched years of these events, I realized that the children on the stage were not looking for just that one person. They were looking for all their support.

I witnessed children who knew their parents would not be sitting by each other if they were divorced. It didn't matter to that child; it only mattered that they were both there. There were times when a child would see most of their family there, but someone they had expected to come didn't show up. I could see honest sadness in their little faces. Each person they expected to be there was just as important as the next one. It didn't matter to that child what had happened on the job that day, or how hard it was for the person to make it there on time. Sometimes, I could even watch them mouth their concern from the stage. That child was getting the message that they were not important, or certainly not as important as whatever was keeping that person away. I wondered why the child didn't know they weren't coming and I wished there was a way for that missing person to understand the hurtful message that child received.

> *Give your child the gift of your time. Being there makes them feel empowered. If you can't be there, just be honest.*

Our extended family didn't live close by so they didn't attend the girls' events. Once in the while, their grandparents would be visiting and then the girls would be thrilled to finally have a grandparent in attendance! But most of the time, it was just our small family there to support them. I felt bad that most of the other children had extended family there, but that was just the way it was. The girls knew it, but as large groups of people would gather around a child after an event, I would feel bad it was just us. That is why it was so important to me to have the girls attend each other's events. As they got older and had other responsibilities, it became harder for them to do that, but I still kept pushing for them to be there.

I was not always successful. Ashley doesn't feel empathy and was a little too honest. She could not understand what difference it made if she went to her sister's choir concerts or not. If she went, she would let everyone know she only went because we made her go. Years later, Lindsey shared her desire to have Ashley come to her last high school choir concert when Ashley was home from college. Lindsey even pointed out all the band concerts she attended for Ashley. Ashley argued she had attended a choir concert over spring break and they were just so long. She wanted to know if I was going to make her go. I said no, secretly hoping she would want to go. I even told Ashley that Lindsey cried when I told her she wasn't going to go. She just didn't get it. The first question Lindsey asked after the concert was, "Did Ashley come?"

It still breaks my heart that Ashley hurt Lindsey with her lack of support. I hope someday she will understand that just by attending an event she would have let Lindsey know she was important to her. She couldn't understand that because Lindsey was the youngest, she only had Mom and Dad at her events for two years; no sisters, because they were off at college. It didn't matter that she had been to one event. Lindsey had been to every one of Ashley's senior band and jazz band concerts she could attend. When Lindsey was a senior, she only had Mom and Dad at her events. Just being there says, 'I love you'.

> *You can't force a child to feel empathy, but you should tell them how they make others feel.*

Engaged Audience

As the world of technology changed when the girls were in high school, people were at these events, but still not fully present; they were on their portable devices. As I attended Lindsey's high school events, I was amazed at the number of phone calls I would hear happening around me. I can't even remember the number of phones I heard ring or beep, which I could ignore. But more than a few times people actually did pick up their phones and talk on them. I would rudely stare at them in hopes they would get the message. At one concert, the director put up a screen presentation telling those in the audience the proper way to behave. Seriously, some didn't get it, even with that! I wondered what the performing teenager thought of their parents' behavior. It didn't take long before I witnessed my answer.

I was at Lindsey's softball game and one of her team members stepped out of the batter's box to turn to her mom to say, "Your phone is ringing!" She had recognized the ring tone.

After that same game, I overheard an argument between a daughter and her dad. He congratulated her on her big hit during the game. She corrected him that he never saw it. She pointed out he was on the phone behind the bleachers, which he was. He had asked another parent what had happened so he could say he saw it. She knew. The argument ended with her telling her dad not to come if he couldn't watch the game.

At Lindsey's last high school concerts, I watched the teenagers on stage look out into the audience. They weren't just looking to see if their parent were there. Now they were looking to see if their parent's eyes were on them or on their electronic devices. I could see in their faces that it mattered if they were focused on them. They wanted to know they were more important than whatever else was happening on their phones. Truly physically being there didn't count anymore. If they were there, but focused on something else, they were sending a painful message: "I know this moment is important to you. That is why I came, but it's not quite as important to me as what I have on my phone."

> *Give your child your undivided attention.*
> *They can tell when you are multi-tasking.*

Electronic devices were popular distractions for siblings in the audience. As parents drag young children along to support their siblings, it is easier if they have something to keep them entertained. Those electronic devices work perfectly, but again the person on stage can tell if they are being ignored. I can remember once a child from the stage pointing at her brother and then pointing at herself, with hand motions, telling him, "Hey, watch me!"

Sharing our Mission: Faith

Being a parent often felt like I was on display and that seemed to intensify at church. As a new mom, it was great to be on display; I loved showing off my beautiful baby . . . until the baby screamed. Then it seemed like the whole congregation was turning their heads around and judging my mothering ability. That's when I would wonder if we should just put the baby into the nursery. Dan and I questioned this decision often, but Jesus' words spoke to us through the Bible[6], "Let the children come to me," (Matthew 19:14a). We decided that we wanted them to be in church with us. When they were little, we took turns walking out of the service with one or the other. Ashley always seemed to need her morning nap right in the middle of service and since she couldn't be laid down in her crib to sleep, she wanted to be walked around. We took turns walking her in the hallway of the church. During times like this, our decision to keep the girls with us during church service waivered. Each of the girls spent at least one Sunday in the nursery. Danielle was fine the first time, but the next time we took her she didn't want to go back. When we tried Ashley in the nursery, she cried the whole time. Lindsey loved playing in the nursery so much we worried she would never want to return to church service. So we went back to our first decision to keep them at church service with us.

There were times when things didn't go as planned. At a Christmas Eve candle light service, I was holding my candle and Lindsey was in my arms and she was smiling at the candle. I just knew that when I had to blow it out, it was going to be a problem, so I waited as long as possible. Everyone else had blown out their candles. We had finished the song. The Pastor was just ready to walk down the aisle, and I blew out my candle. Lindsey screamed. The Pastor said, "Just like in the manger, a babe cries!"

As the girls got older, we started taking snacks to church to entertain them. At first we went with the standard snack a Ziploc bag filled with Cheerios. That seemed to encourage screaming fits of who was going to hold the bag, as well as snacks flying all over the church floor. I did, however, make the girls help pick up all of the Cheerios before we left the pew, hopefully teaching them to respect the church property. Juice boxes seemed to be another disaster, with the juice shooting out of the straw as I tried to hand it to the girls. After several attempts, I finally figured out a solution. They each had their own bag of cut up apples and a fancy cup that we used only for water. No more little Cheerios got dropped, and any spilled beverage was just water that could dry. (Getting out the door for church involved peeling and cutting up three apples, putting each in a separate bag, finding and filling three water cups, and packing them into our diaper bag. This, in addition to getting three girls dressed and their hair done!) That often led to *me* having a yelling fit, "Girls, let's go. It's time to get into the car, now! We are late! I said let's go, hurry!"

Finally, we were heading down the road to church. Often someone was in tears; many times it was me just from the stress. On one morning, I started to wonder if going to church was even worth it. Why bother? Then I realized I needed a different attitude. It wasn't about getting stuff ready; it was about where we were going. Yes, I *did* need a different attitude. I told the whole family that before we got to church, we needed to throw the grumpies out the window. I rubbed my face with both hands and then clasped them together and combined the grumpies into one hand, holding on tightly. I rolled down the window and threw out the imaginary grumpies that I held tightly in my other hand and quickly rolled up the window, yelling at the window to hurry to close before the grumpies came back. Danielle quickly said she had grumpies, so I had her hand me her grumpies since the minivan didn't have a window in back that she could open. Ashley and Lindsey quickly joined in. I had all of the girls' grumpies in my hand. I opened my window and threw them all out, just as I had mine. Of course the girls were quick to point out that Dad didn't throw out his grumpies. He said he didn't have any. (Truth be told, we were both mad at each other, which started my bad mood in the first place.) Filled with my silliness, we all said, "Yes, you do, Dad. Throw out your grumpies."

Dan joined in and not only threw out his grumpies, but pretended to drive fast to get away from them because they were starting to catch up. By the time we arrived at church, we were all in better moods. The little fight Dan and I were in the midst of was long forgotten. It was a much better way to attend church.

Added to the church bag of snacks was a little toy and a book for each girl. Then I wondered why I didn't just have some of these packets at church. That's when I suggested to our church that we have children's packets. I figured if these packets were working for my girls, why not share the idea with other parents? Each packet was a Ziploc plastic bag with a few crayons, a few blank sheets of papers to color on, a book, and a little toy. Then I didn't have to bring one from home for each girl each week. All the girls had to do was grab one as we walked into church on Sunday. Since it was my idea, I was volunteered to clean them out each week. It actually worked out great because I did it while the older two girls were in the church's preschool. Lindsey, who was two years old, assisted me each week. She would pick her favorite bag and hide it. Then on Sunday morning she would pull it out and was so happy, she had the best bag. (I guess she was taught how to volunteer at a young age, and perhaps the rewards of volunteering!)

The only thing we didn't like about our church was there were not many little children in the church service. The church had Sunday school during two worship hours, which worked for us. We attended church and then the older girls went to Sunday school afterwards.

However, most parents went to church while their children were in Sunday school. I realized it was just an option, but it made me question our way. I recognized attending church as a family was a very strong value of mine. I understood it was because I grew up attending church with my mom, but not my dad. My dad was more of a casual church attendee, but my Mom guided and shaped my faith. I always wished our whole family was at church together, so I decided the girls would always be attending church with Dan and me. It was a core value of mine more than it was a logical decision. So the girls continued to attend church with us since we were through the roughest years anyway. The older two went to Sunday school after church, which they loved, because it was fun. There were stories, a craft, and music.

Dan and I took turns entertaining Lindsey during the Sunday school hour. Lindsey always wanted to do what her sisters did, so she would get mad because she couldn't go to Sunday school like her sisters. When Lindsey was just 30 months old, I asked if she could start the 3-year-old Sunday school class. She could if I taught it. (What a great way to get a new teacher.) Since I had been a teacher, I figured I would do it. It was crazy and I quickly learned I was *not* a preschool teacher. I recruited Dan's help and the two of us taught a Sunday school class for three-year-olds that year. A few other times I taught Sunday school, but each time I was reminded that even though I had been a high school teacher, I didn't have enough patience for the younger grades. Dan, on the other hand, did teach the girls in their confirmation classes. It meant a lot to me that he was sharing his faith with the girls at such an important time in their lives, since it was not something my dad had done for me.

✧ ✧ ✧

Faith was incorporated into our family life with the traditional bedtime prayer that was on a plaque in the girls' nursery. "Now I lay me down to sleep, I pray the Lord my soul to keep. May the angels watch me through the night, and wake me with the morning light. Amen." It was time to add a table grace. I searched at the Christian bookstore and found a book on prayers. I picked a fun dinner table grace appropriate for their age. We started saying it every time all five of us were gathered around the table for dinner, but I never thought it would last forever. They still say the same silly grace today when we have family dinner! "Thank you for the food we eat. Thank you for the world so sweet. Thank you for the birds that sing. Thank you, God, for everything, Amen."[7]

> *Teach your values to your children in your everyday life, not just on Sundays or in public.*

It didn't take long for the girls to memorize these prayers, and that's when I realized they had not learned the Lord's Prayer they had been saying for years at church. As I watched them during the church service, they were quiet and entertained, but now it was time for them to learn to participate in the service. I taught them to stop what they were doing, fold their hands, and sit quietly while we said the Lord's Prayer. Soon they started saying it with us, just from hearing it over and over. Little Lindsey started creating very cute words in her prayer: "who's art heaven, how thy name."

There were still times in church when I felt like everyone was turning around to see what all the noise was about. Whenever there is an almost three-year-old in the family, it's a guarantee there will be noise. When I saw all the heads turn around, I still felt like they were all judging my mothering ability. I would whisper to the girls, "Look . . . everyone is watching you."

Naturally, they would look up. It never failed someone had turned around to look. (Often it was another kid, but it worked.) The older girls didn't want others to see them crying or throwing a fit, so they would quiet down. That didn't work for Lindsey. She loved getting the attention of others, so having everyone turn around to see her misbehave was her motivation, so I decided it was time to move the family up to the second pew of the church. Now when Lindsey acted up, no one turned around to see her; they could see it as it happened.

As it turned out, all three of them were better behaved. The girls could see what was going on up front. We had several members of the church tell us we were either brave or crazy. I didn't think it mattered since I had always thought I was getting judged on my mothering ability in the back of the church anyway, so at least now they could truly see what I was doing.

Since we were sitting up front, it was time for Ashley

and Danielle to stand at the appropriate spots. Once the girls were in school and were learning to read, they had to stand and follow along. Lindsey would get to color while Danielle was following along in the hymnal. When she would question why she couldn't color like her sister, I would explain that it was because she was in first grade and Lindsey was in preschool. They did what was appropriate for their age.

It became obvious that the girls were all listening in church when they had questions I couldn't answer, so I would ask Dan if he knew. If he didn't, then together we would search in the Bible for the answer. We even bought a Children's Bible, which helped us share the stories with the girls more easily. But one time they had a question we couldn't find.

> *Be honest with your child; if you don't know the answer, seek it out together.*

"What is Noah's wife's name?"

Neither Dan or I could find the answer, so I had the girls ask our pastor. He explained that many times the women didn't have names, other than the wife of someone, like Noah's wife. The girls were even more confused. So he said he would do some research and see what he could find. He reported back that nowhere is it written what her name is. He again tried to explain that in those times, women didn't have significant enough roles to be given names.

In response to this, they all started reading the Bible

Project Testing

and together made a list of women who *were* named in the Bible. They wanted to prove to the pastor that women were important.

The girls' church involvement grew as they got older. Starting in kindergarten, they could sing in the youth choir at church. Lindsey was always challenged to wait until she was old enough. Each girl went through many rites of passage in the church. They received Children's Bibles in the third grade and had first communion in the fifth grade.

They continued to participate in different youth choirs all the way through high school. The girls each started confirmation classes when they were in seventh grade and were each confirmed in the fall of their tenth grade years.

Dan and I at church with Lindsey, Ashley, and Danielle

The girls' activity in the youth programs at church also became a pillar for them. It started with an activity once a month when the girls were in third through fifth grades. There was another group for them when they were in junior high. I became involved in the youth committee at church that guided the direction of the youth program. Many times, Dan or I would chaperone or be a driver for the different activities. The girls enjoyed being with their friends at church and liked having activities they did without their siblings. They could only attend their age group's activity and one parent would stay home with the other girls.

One summer, Danielle and Ashley were attending a two-week camp and had a Parent Day. Dan and I were excited to attend. We toured the camp and participated in an outdoor church service. Standing in the back, watching the girls lead worship and sing glory to God touched my soul. On our way home, Dan admitted that he now understood why I pushed for camp and all of the church activities. It was not something he had done as a child and he supported me in my desire to have them involved. But on that day, he understood what we were accomplishing. Our girls were building their faith and sharing it with others.

In high school, the girls were even more involved with the youth activities. They didn't want their parents around, but they understood that there had to be adult supervision besides just the youth director. That meant some of the time it would have to be me. Occasionally, there were activities Dan and I were not ready to let the girls participate in, like a mission trip to Mexico. Danielle really wanted to go, but Dan was entirely against it, so the compromise was that I would have to go with her. As it turned out, most teenagers who attended had their parents chaperone. It was such a moving experience for both Danielle and me, so when the opportunity came around again, I encouraged Dan to chaperone with Ashley and Danielle. The girls also went to New Orleans and Texas, but the most meaningful trip was a local mission adventure where they witnessed the needs of people in their own community. I am sure the girls participated in their first mission trip for the fun of hanging out with friends, but when they returned, they were changed. They gained a strong mission-giving heart and soul. They continue to serve to this day.

> *Be a charitable family. That value will be ingrained into your child's life.*

In the Rearview Mirror of Project Testing

Looking back, I treasure the relationships I have made with other parents. I loved being able to offer a solution to another mom's struggles. I remember a time when some of my friends asked if I had struggled with postpartum depression. I hadn't, but I asked why they were asking. They had a friend they were worried about who just had her second child and was struggling. She also needed a spare crib if I knew anyone. I had the crib, so I reached out to her. When I delivered the crib, I realized she just needed a friend; it didn't matter that I had not gone through the same things she was going through. She just needed someone. She ended up being one of my best friends. I guess sometimes all we need is to be willing to listen.

The harder challenge was to reach out when I needed help. Many times I was forced into it, because

I just couldn't do it all with three girls. But it was easier to give to others than it was to ask others to help me. It was an important lesson to learn because it does take collaboration to raise a child. The girls were not raised in a vacuum; they were very much a part of society, the good and bad of people.

When our child had her first school program, we were so proud, we couldn't image missing it. In a few years, we realized we had two programs per child, per year, to attend. That was six programs a year and they were not all even in school yet. I would love to tell you that each and every program was so unique and meaningful, but they kind of blended together. I started to question if both parents had to attend every program. Dan was the one who pointed out that it wasn't about us. It was very important to our daughter! He reminded me to be a loyal supportive parent. He not only spent hours sitting alongside of me in the audience of dance recitals (even going on stage for one), band, and choir concerts, but he also would attend and help at practices and games of T-ball, baseball, softball, volleyball, and basketball. He was the proud daddy!

Church turned out to be a cornerstone of our family. It wasn't something I planned would happen when we became parents. It is something that grew over time. In church, the girls shared their musical talent; we all made friends and gained a giving spirit. My faith grew as I witnessed God's presence in the girls. I was supported by that faith every day as I struggled with doing the right thing as a mom. I leaned on that faith to trust that God would keep the girls safe.

Section III:
WORKING MYSELF OUT OF A JOB

Chapter 8:
Letting Her Do It

I found one of the hardest jobs of being a mom was allowing my children to do things on their own. Many times, it was just much easier to do whatever it was myself. I was actually forced into giving them some independence because with three girls so close together in age, I couldn't be in three places at once. Out of necessity I had to let them learn and try things on their own. Sometimes that meant I had to let them fail.

At the Table

Before Danielle could talk, she was already saying with her actions, *'Me do it.'* I would be feeding her baby food and she would grab at the spoon. At first it was a game. I would win if I got the food to her mouth before she could grab the spoon and she would win if she got ahold of the spoon and waved it around. It was a tie if she got the spoon after I got food to her mouth. At first I won more than she did, and then when she started to win more than I did, baby food was going everywhere.

This was not a game I chose to play, but it was a favorite of Danielle's.

> *Relax and be willing to play the feed-the-baby game; remember to be patient.*

At first I handed her an extra spoon, which she loved. That meant our new game was for me to try to get my spoon full of food to her mouth without getting hit with her spoon. That worked for about a week, that is, until Danielle became proficient at finding her mouth with her spoon. Then I would have to take her spoon out of her mouth, put my spoonful into her mouth and hand her back her empty spoon. That worked until she realized her spoon was not getting any food to her mouth. She would drop her empty spoon as fast as I could hand it to her and grab my spoon again. Now her eye hand coordination was more developed so she was winning this game more than I was. Finally, I realized I had to let her hold part of the spoon and strongly guide her hand and spoon to her mouth. It was always so frustrating to not be able to just shovel the baby food into her mouth myself. I admit that I attempted to hold her hands down many times . . . and sometimes it worked.

It was a great day when she could start to eat finger foods. She loved to spend her time carefully picking up each piece. While she was doing that, I could sneak a few spoonfuls of baby food into her mouth. That, too, worked for about a week, until she was now saying something that sounded like, "Me do it."

Turned out, Danielle wanted to **only** eat foods she could put into her mouth herself. I had to cut up her food as small as possible so she could pick them up. That worked for a week until she needed more food options. She was not going to let me use the spoon, so I had to hand the spoon over to her. It was time to let her do it! All of this took much longer and was so much messier than I would have liked, but she did it herself!

Simpler games were played out in many ways as she continued to learn to feed herself. Thankfully, each stage seemed to only last a week. When she was two years old, we moved Danielle from the highchair to the booster chair and I repeated the whole process with Ashley. This time it seemed less stressful to move from one stage to the next, probably because I knew the games we would play. In the end, she would win and I would lose. When Ashley was two, we moved her into the booster chair as Danielle, three, moved to a regular chair. It was now my turn to repeat the process with Lindsey, and this time, it seemed even less stressful. It could have been because I was more experienced, was used to the messes (which was even bigger now with the two older girls), or I was too busy to play the games.

Lindsey loved to stay in her high chair, and sat there, slowly feeding herself finger foods until all of us were done eating supper. I guess it was easier to let her to do it herself!

At the table, *'Me do it'* was scary to hear. I looked up to see Danielle, then four years old, reaching for the applesauce jar to pour more into her bowl. (We had given up on spooning applesauce out of the jar and would just pour it into three bowls for the girls. It was much faster.) I had been grabbing things out of Danielle's hand for a few weeks, so I knew it was time to let her try. She carefully and slowly poured it into her bowl. Success!

Not to be left out, Ashley said, "Me do it."

Since it worked with Danielle and I wasn't up for a temper tantrum, I gave in. But before I had time to grab the jar out of her hand, Ashley's bowl was buried beneath about two cups of apple sauce. I quickly grabbed two bowls and spoons from the kitchen as Ashley started to cry. Into one extra bowl, I scraped the applesauce from the table and handed it to Dan. I took Ashley's bowl and poured out half of it into the other extra bowl. Ashley was worried I was taking her applesauce away, but I quickly set her bowl back down in front of her and the other extra bowl at my spot. Then I wiped up the table and sat back down at my spot.

I said, "Oh no, accidents happen. I guess Daddy and I needed some applesauce for supper."

Ashley was in shock that she wasn't in trouble. I didn't get mad; I just reacted to her fear. As she saw what happened, she was scared she was in trouble, but I didn't want her to be afraid of a little accident at the table, so I just cleaned it up quickly. I have to admit it was easier for me to react that way because it was all contained on the table. The next time she tried, I remembered and had a guiding hand above the jar, preventing it from being tipped more than a 90-degree angle. Then I told her to pour slowly. Ashley successfully poured it slowly into her bowl. She did it **herself!**

At our table, milk was the item that was poured the most. The milk jug had a safe place next to Dan's chair on the floor. We had learned to put it on the floor after many attempts of little hands trying to grab it at the table. A gallon of milk being spilled was something we were going to prevent, no matter what. So whenever someone wanted more milk, it was Dan's job. That worked for what seemed like a week, then we started to hear, "Me do it!"

"No, Daddy will do it," was his answer. That is, until Danielle decided she wouldn't have any milk unless she could pour it. That wasn't going to change Dan's mind, so she went without more milk.

The next night, I saw both Ashley and Danielle successfully pouring applesauce from the plastic applesauce jar. I got an idea. After dinner I washed up the empty applesauce jar and approached Dan.

"Do you think the girls could start to pour their own milk from this?" I held up the plastic applesauce jar.

"I guess it's worth a try," he said. "They don't want me to pour their milk anymore."

The next night, I poured their cups of milk and filled the empty applesauce jar half-full of milk. Ashley didn't like that. Milk goes in the gallon container and applesauce goes in the applesauce jar . . . but I ignored her complaint. The applesauce jar with milk in it sat on the table. It wasn't long into the meal when Lindsey needed more milk. Dan, out of habit, reached for the gallon container on the floor. I stopped him and poured Lindsey some more milk from the applesauce jar. Danielle got it, and she quickly finished drinking up her milk and asked for more. With anticipation on all of our faces, she said, "Me do it."

I handed her the applesauce jar that was now less than half-filled with milk. Dan told her to pour slowly, and that the milk would come out faster than the applesauce did. She *almost* did it herself. Dan had to stop her from pouring too much milk into her cup, but no milk was spilled. She beamed with her independence; she did it **herself!**

Ashley still didn't like milk being in an applesauce jar. When she wanted more milk, we let her decide which container she wanted. Of course she wanted the milk jug, **and** she wanted to pour it herself. Both Dan and I quickly denied that request. She had to decide to drink milk from the jug with Dan pouring, or she could pour from the applesauce jar. Of course milk could only come from the milk jug, so that was the end of that.

Several days later, Ashley happened to see me pouring milk from the jug into the applesauce jar. She was so excited to learn how it got there. Only then was she ready to accept milk from the applesauce jar—and she was so excited she could pour her milk **herself!**

Of course there were many nights of spilled milk. I seemed to handle it quickly and without much fuss when it was contained to the table, but when milk went onto the child, the chair, and the floor, I was angry. Several times I yelled about not paying attention, someone being careless, or even why did it always happen on the day I had mopped the floor. By the time I was finished cleaning up and I had made someone cry, I would realize it was an accident and I had overreacted. I would look at the sad child and say, "Oh no, accidents happen, and I forgot that! I am so sorry I got upset over just an accident and it's no one's fault. Will you forgive me for yelling at you?"

They would nod and I would give them a hug.

There was one time when an entire gallon of milk was spilled onto the floor. This time *I* had dropped it and I yelled at myself while both Dan and I cleaned it up. He tried to say, "Oh no, accidents happen . . . " just as I would say to the children, but I couldn't and wouldn't calm down. I was mad as I saw an entire gallon of milk splayed out on the floor like white paint! By the time I sat down at the table to eat, everyone was silent and scared. I finally felt the tension I had caused.

I exhaled and said to all of them, "Oh no, accidents happen. I am so sorry for yelling at myself for spilling the milk. I forgot it was just an accident! Accidents happen and it's no one's fault. Should I forgive myself for yelling at me?"

The girls all nodded and I gave each of them a hug. I even gave Dan a kiss for helping me clean up the milk and a hug for trying to calm me down. He said, "Oh no, accidents happen."

> *Accidents are a way of life with children. Remember that when you can, but don't beat yourself up when you overreact.*

Getting Dressed

It was a good thing I had three girls close together in age; otherwise, I think I would still be dressing them when they went to kindergarten. It was so much easier for me to put their clothes on for them than it was to wait for them to struggle through the process and still need me to help them. I just didn't have enough hands for them at the same time, so I had to let go of the control and let them learn to do it themselves!

It all started with getting ready for bed. As I finished snapping up Lindsey's sleeper, in walked Ashley. Just as I got started helping her, Danielle, then three, appeared in the doorway. Dan was still in the bathroom draining the tub and cleaning up the bathtime mess. I knew he would be there to help me in a minute, so I gave Ashley, then two, her pajama pants and set her on the floor. I thought she would just sit there and wait for her dad to put them on for her. I began to help Danielle into her pajamas. Before I knew what happened, Ashley was screaming as she tried to put both legs into one leg of her pajamas and had gotten stuck. Meanwhile, Danielle was yelling at me, "Me do it!"

As Dan hurried into the room, I was ignoring Danielle and getting Ashley out of her pajamas. I comforted Ashley and explained one leg had to go into one side of the pajamas. At the same time, Dan was attempting to let

Letting Her Do It

Danielle do it herself. He did learn from Ashley's attempt to be sure she was putting one leg into one side of the pants and the other leg into the other, but as she stepped into the bottoms, she was holding on to his shoulder. She was successful and very proud of her accomplishment, but as I watched out of the corner of my eye, I had a vision of our future and all three girls trying to hold a shoulder as they balanced to put on their pajamas. Since I had only two shoulders, that wasn't going to work.

Later that night, I decided to dig into my parenting books and check out ideas for teaching my toddlers how to dress themselves. The first thing I found was that we had moved into a new stage: the 'Me Do It' stage. As I read the chapter, I realized this stage was on top of me and I had not even noticed. Danielle was trying more and more things when I was busy with her sisters. I just thought it was because I was busy. No . . . it was because she was a toddler and wanted to do it **herself**.

I picked up a few helpful hints in my books. Toddlers will attempt to do more than they physically can and will get frustrated with their failure. When you help them, they get mad because you took it away from them and they experience a feeling of failure. The key, according to the parenting books, was to try to let them finish tasks, so their last attempt was successful. The example the book gave was to start a zipper for them, but let them finish the zip. Then you could say, *'You did it,'* and congratulate them.

The next day I started to focus on the end of every task I did for Danielle. When she was getting dressed, I pulled her pants up to her knees and let her finish them.

A Mommy's Road

I put her shirt on and she pulled it on the rest of the way. Each time I would smile and say, "You did it!"

And each time, she beamed with excitement! Not long after the pajama incident, once, as we were getting ready to leave the house, I heard Danielle yelling. She was in the closet, mad that she couldn't reach her coat. I pulled it down for her and off she ran, saying, "Me do it!"

Busy with getting the coats on the other two and trying to get us all out the door, I didn't pay any attention to Danielle. She was still crying and screaming. When I finally got to her, she had her coat on upside down and was screaming that she couldn't zip it. I had to bite the inside of my cheeks not to laugh because it looked so funny. Her frustration level was so high and she was so mad. I didn't want to make her feel like a failure, but she had her coat on upside down! I tried to get her to come to me, but she refused; she was too mad. Ashley started to point out her coat was wrong and I knew that would really send Danielle into a tailspin, so I intervened and said, "Is that coat of yours giving you trouble?"

> *Sometimes you just need a crazy idea to get through a situation. It doesn't always need to make sense.*

Danielle gave me the strangest look. I went on to blame the coat for giving her trouble. I told her to take off her coat and give it a time-out for being bad. She continued to look at me with this strange look, but she let me grab her and take off the coat. As I finished taking off the coat, I talked to it. I called it a bad coat for giving Danielle trouble. I asked the coat if it was ready to behave this time. Danielle was still wondering what I was doing and let me guide her arms into the sleeves as I talked to her coat. Finally, I started the zipper and let her finish zipping it up. I gave her a big hug and said, "See, if your coat is good, you can do it!"

She smiled as I wiped her tears away. The book was right; the end was the most important thing!

As the day continued, I realized I had missed all the signs of this new stage. Danielle was trying to do so many things on her own. I kept hearing, "Me do it!"

As I started the bedtime routine, I remembered my vision of all three girls holding my shoulder to put on their pajama pants, so I told Danielle to sit down on the floor. I laid her pajamas over her legs and I explained how we should peek inside our pajama bottoms to look for the tag. I told her that the tag should be looking up at her. If she didn't see the tag, we needed to flip them over. We flipped her pajamas a few times until she had it figured out. Then I had her slide her legs into her pajama bottoms. She tried to stand up with her toes at the knees of the pants so she had to lean on my shoulders to get the pants up. It took me a few nights to figure out she had to slide her pants all the way over her toes and then stand up. She just couldn't understand why, so I had to demonstrate. I took her into my room while I put on my pajamas. I did it exactly the way I was teaching her to do it herself. I sat down on the floor and put my feet in the pajamas. When I stood up with them still covering my toes, I fell down. I tried again and I fell down. Then Danielle said, "You have to see your toes first."

I tried again, asking her as I went. When she saw my toes sticking out of the bottom of the pajama pants, she told me to stand up. So I stood up, asking if I would fall again. She shook her head. This time, I stood up and pulled up my pants without falling. "You did it," she gleamed.

After that demonstration, she always remembered to first see her toes, and *then* she could easily stand up. Now she was putting her pajamas on by herself, always ending with an, "I did it!"

As you might imagine, pajamas were much easier to put on than clothes. As the months went by, there were many mornings that were filled with frustration. I would try to help Danielle get to the last step and then let her finish up so she could feel successful. Sometimes her frustration level would get too high, though, and I couldn't help. Then it was always the clothes' fault. We would call the shirt a name, or throw it on the floor. Once in a while we wouldn't wear that shirt if it was going to cause so much trouble.

That winter, I watched a preschooler put on his coat at church one day and his method amazed me! He had laid his coat down in front of him upside down, bent down, put his arms in, and then flipped it over his head. It looked silly, but it worked. I was staring, so his mom noticed me and told me he had learned it at preschool. I asked how it worked, so she had him proudly demonstrate it to me. I hadn't realized he had to stand at the neck of the jacket to get it to end right-side-up, so I was glad to see him do it a second time. He was able to do it all by himself and was proud of his accomplishment.

When we got home, I wanted Danielle give it a try, but she didn't want to lay her coat on the floor. And besides that, she wasn't going anywhere and we had just gotten home. As I tried to persuade her to give it a try, Dan said he would try it.

I explained the procedure to Dan. He laid his coat on the floor and was standing at the bottom of his coat. I told him to stand at the collar and he argued it would be upside down. I smiled and just encouraged him to try it. I told him to bend down and put his arms in the sleeves and flip the coat over his head. He did . . . and it worked.

Ashley thought that looked silly, but it was a cool game so she said, "Me do it!"

I laid her coat out on the floor upside down in front of where she was standing. I pointed to the sleeves and said, "Put your hands in here."

She did, and I helped her flip the coat over her head. It worked and she loved it. In fact, she was so excited that she asked to do it again.

Finally Danielle was willing to give it a try, but was standing at the bottom of the coat and fell into it because she couldn't reach the armholes. Dan explained, "Mommy's idea is backwards, but it works. When you look at the coat it has to look upside down."

As Dan guided her to the correct side of the coat,

she laughed as she repeated, "Mommy is backwards."
Under my breath, I said, "Thanks, Dan."
But he pointed out, "It worked, didn't it?" I agreed…

> *Humor is so very important, even at your own expense.*

Now I was thrilled to have the process of getting out of the house be a little easier. I could hand Danielle her coat and she could flip it over her head. I would lay Ashley's coat at her feet and she would flip it on. I was then able to put Lindsey in her coat. I would grab Ashley to put the two ends of her zipper together and hold the bottom while she zipped it up. She did it, and then I had two girls ready. I would turn to Danielle and see how she was doing with her coat; sometimes she was patiently still working on her zipper. Then I would put my coat on. I would then turn back to Danielle, who was by now getting frustrated that the two ends of her zipper wouldn't go together. I pointed out her zipper was being stubborn and might need a little mommy help today. Whenever that happened, I would put the two ends together and guide her hand to hold the bottom of the zipper as she zipped up her coat with the other hand. She did it, and now I had all three girls ready to go.

The coat was just the beginning of the 'Me do it' stage for Ashley. I think she was determined to do everything her sister was able to do, so that stage came on for her fast and furious. Many mornings, I would run to a screaming Ashley as she was stuck with her head in

Letting Her Do It

her shirt. Either her head was bigger than Danielle's, or she just couldn't find the sweet spot to pull the shirt over her head, but she was always able to finish pulling her shirt down over her tummy, so I could say, "You did it!"

Lindsey was not about to be left out of doing things on her own. One day during her naptime, when I had thought she was long asleep, she started yelling– she was mad. I ran up the stairs, only to see her standing in her crib with most of her clothes off. She was standing there, holding onto the bottom of her shirt with one hand and the side of the crib with the other . . . she had attempted to put her shirt back on as her pants. I bit the inside of my cheek to keep from laughing and asked, "What's wrong?"

She demonstrated by letting go of her shirt and it fell to her ankles. She was mad that her shirt wouldn't work as her pants. I said, "Oh no, it won't stay up. But where is your diaper?"

Since she had already pulled her shirt back up, she peeked down at her bottom and saw she was missing her diaper. Surprised, she looked around and pointed at her diaper on the other side of her crib.

With a giggle, I explained I would be right back. I had to grab my camera to get a picture of this moment.

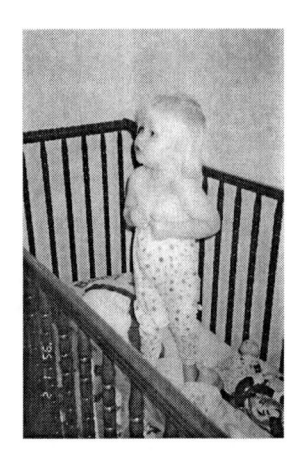

Lindsey napping?

She had spent this whole time, when I thought

she was sleeping, carefully taking off her socks, pants, diaper, and shirt. I had never seen her take off anything but her socks before. She was able to do all of that without frustration. She would have been able to put her pants on correctly if she had tried them first instead of her shirt. I lucked out there, since she would have been dressed without a diaper! I quickly snapped a picture and asked, "Should we get your diaper back on?"

She agreed that would be a good idea. Then I held up both her shirt and her pants and told her we would put this one, the shirt, over her head. She smiled. Then I picked up her pants and said, "Let's try this one on your legs."

I had her stand up and pull up her pants, as I asked, "Do they work?"

"Yeah!" she cheered. She was happy to do the last part.

Lindsey continued to do her own undressing, but mostly at bath time. She always seemed to start things at a much younger age than her sisters. Was it that she was an advanced child, just more independent, or was I just a more relaxed mom? Perhaps it was a combination of all three, but Lindsey continued to start at an early age and was not to be left out of whatever her sisters were able to do.

Mommy Fix It

Even though I learned that finishing tasks made the girls feel successful, I couldn't leave well enough alone. When the girls were dressed, I would tweak their outfits. I would look down and see their clothes were on backwards; they had to be fixed, didn't they? I was even correcting their pajamas! Wow, I was really still controlling them and taking away their accomplishment, just so their clothes were on right! I would see their excitement of getting dressed all by themselves disappear as I fixed their outfits. I always seemed to notice what I was doing when I was in the middle of correcting an outfit, but by then it was too late.

> *How your child feels about their accomplishment is more important than how they look.*

I had to force myself to stop and think. Then I asked myself if we were even leaving the house. One day I ended up asking the question out loud without realizing it. "Does it matter if Barney is on the back?"

Ashley heard me ask and looked down at her tummy and said, "Where is Barney?"

I pointed to her back. I asked if she wanted to fix it. She said, "Yes, I need to see Barney."

I hadn't even thought of letting them make the decision of changing their clothes; I was just doing it for them because I thought it needed to be done. So I started asking them if it mattered and they were able to decide for themselves. I was learning to be proud of my girls' accomplishments, even if their clothing was on backwards. When another adult would point out something was on backwards, I was able to brush it off. I told myself that I was developing independent, confident children. That was much more important than if their clothes were on backwards or not. That worked until someone pointed out that if Ashley wore her shoes on the wrong feet, it could affect her walking. I had no idea if that was even true, but I didn't want her to have to wear corrective shoes like I did as a child. I decided she needed to be more successful on getting her shoes on the right feet.

That began with me pointing out the shape of the shoe to Ashley, but she couldn't see a difference. To her, they both looked the same. Each time they were wrong, I would help her change them. Even Danielle was starting to point out when her shoes were on the wrong feet. Ashley got mad and stopped putting her shoes on because, "I can't do it right!"

I needed a simple way to help her be successful again. I got a red marker and put a circle on the inside edge of each shoe. As I put her shoes on, I pointed out the new circles. I told her, "Your shoes like each other so when you put them on, the red marks have to kiss."

First, I put them on correctly. I showed her how they kiss when she stood up. We tried again. This time, I put them on wrong. When she stood up, I asked her, "Do your shoes kiss?"

"No," she said. She sat down again and we fixed them. Sometimes, I would see her putting on and taking off her shoes to get them right. She still couldn't see which shoe was which before she put them on, but she could switch them without anyone having to point out her mistake. If she forgot to check, I would just ask, "Are your shoes mad at each other? They are not kissing."

She would sit down and change them right away. She would be so proud of her accomplishment and say, "They like each other now... they are kissing!"

In the Rearview Mirror of Letting Her Do It

Looking back, I know that when I was busy or stressed, I was only focused on getting 'it' done. I didn't see the girls' sadness or look of failure in their eyes when I was too focused on my own needs and the task that had to be completed. When I was relaxed, it was easy to see their eagerness to do 'it' themselves. It was fun to see them get excited when they were successful. Making everyday activities a game was so much better than making them chores, especially for the girls.

At the time I blamed the clothes for being bad, I didn't realize I was teaching them how to cope with failure or challenges in their life . . . but I was. I didn't think about their fragile self esteem when I would blame an object for not cooperating instead of blaming them. I was just taking time to look into their eyes, and in those moments, I saw their feelings written all over their faces. Just by taking time, I was able to do the right things.

Chapter 9:
Allowing Independence

At some jobs, it is important to make yourself irreplaceable. When that happens, it improves the chances that you will be able to keep that job forever. However, there are other jobs that your success is evident when you can step away and everything goes on without a hitch. I realized that being a mom was the second one. I had to work myself out of my own job. Then and only then was I going to be a successful mom.

Big Girl Bed

When Ashley was born, we didn't want to disrupt Danielle's excellent sleep pattern by taking her out of her crib, so we purchased a second hand crib and just had two cribs until we were ready to let Danielle have more freedom. When the time came, we started with Danielle (who was almost three) sleeping in our guest bed. We pushed the double bed against the wall and purchased a bed rail to put on the other side of it. The first night, we went through the same bedtime routine with both Danielle and Ashley. While I read to Ashley and put her into her crib, Dan read to Danielle and cuddled with her in her big girl bed. We both waited outside in the hallway for Danielle to get out of her bed. We waited and waited, but she didn't come out. We peeked into her room and saw her all settled down in her big girl bed. The struggle to get her to stay in her bed at night never happened. I don't know if it was our consistent bedtime routine, if it seemed like her crib with the rail on the side, or if she just liked going to sleep at night, but the switch from a crib to a bed was a breeze. She even stayed in her bed all night, just like she did her crib. If she needed us during the night, she would just call us.

And yet, it didn't take long for me to discover the big girl bed challenge. Danielle did get out of bed in the morning when she was done sleeping . . . and Danielle was a very early riser. (I used to wonder if she would ever sleep in when she was a teenager. She did, but now is back to being an early bird.) I would start my day with Danielle standing next to my bed, her cute little nose only a few inches from mine.

"Mommy, time to get up."

At first, I would pull her close to me and give her a hug. Then, I would climb out of bed to start my day. Finally, I would glance at the clock, only to see that it was—on average— 5:15 a.m.! Wait a minute! I was not ready to start my day, but now I was up and awake. Even though I was disheartened at the sleep I was missing out on, Danielle and I would head downstairs to start our morning over an hour earlier than normal. Some mornings I looked at the clock as soon as I felt that cute little nose next to mine. Then if it was too early, I would pull her into bed with us to try to get another hour of sleep. That didn't work because she was awake and ready to play and sing in bed. Now I was awake . . . and so was Dan—at 5:20 a.m.!

I decided I needed some advice, so I did a little research in my parenting books on early-to-rise toddlers. Out of the eight parenting books I had on my shelf (this was before internet), I didn't find *any* information on the subject, so off to the bookstore I went. There, I found information on moving a child to a big bed, how to keep your toddler in a big bed, how to keep your child in a big bed throughout the night . . . but nothing on dealing with an early-to-rise toddler. Great, I had a unique problem. I decided to wait it out. Perhaps, it was just an adjustment phase and soon she would sleep later in the morning.

> *You will have unique problems; to find the solutions, you need to think outside the box.*

Some mornings she did sleep until 6:30 a.m., but other mornings it was closer to 5:00 am. We even tried keeping her up later at night, but that didn't change her wake up time; it just made her cranky all day. What started to change was my attitude. Each morning as I felt that cute little nose next to mine, I would lift my head to look at the clock. What time I saw on the clock determined my mood for the day! I would complain to Dan that I would do anything to be able to get up and have just a few minutes to myself before I started my 'work' day. He got to get up, get showered, eat breakfast, and drive to his job before his day started. I only had time to open my eyes! Sometimes he would wisely just say he was sorry and give me a hug. Other mornings during my complaints, he would remind me that he could stay home and I could work at an outside job. Then one day, he pointed out that it really wasn't Danielle's fault she couldn't read a clock and know when I wanted her to get up. His comment gave me serious pause, and pushed my creative mind in the right direction.

Danielle was at the age where she did recognize numbers. She could learn to read a digital clock. I found a spare digital clock and I put it on the nightstand near her bed. Danielle and I started to play with her new clock. I told her she had to stay in her big girl bed until her new clock said 6:00. I moved the numbers so it said 5:58 and we waited together for it to turn 6:00. And I would tell her it was now time to get up. We repeated it, this time pretending to sleep. At 5:59, I asked her if it was time to get up and she shook her head, no. Then when it turned 6:00 she said, "Get up now!"

"Yes," I said. "Exactly right!" I explained how this was only when it was dark outside and when Daddy was home, but not at nap time. At nap time, she could get up when she was done sleeping. But when Mommy and Daddy were sleeping, she had to wait until her new clock said 6:00. She understood, and we agreed that she would only look at the clock when it was dark out.

I wanted her to be successful from the very beginning. It was going to be a training process and I didn't want to make her bed a punishment. (Yes, I got that from all those chapters on sleeping.) I actually set the clock one hour ahead, so at 5:00 in the morning, the clock said 6:00. Since she sometimes woke up that early, I wanted her to still be successful. The very first morning, she came next to my bed and said, "Mommy, it's time to get up, I saw the 6!"

"Congratulations, you slept to 6:00!" I said as I gave her a big hug. Yes, I was getting up again at 5:15 a.m., but I knew this was going to be a process. I felt hopeful that we would get there. So each day, I moved the clock five minutes to get it closer to the actual time.

On the third morning, I was awakened in the middle of the night with Danielle standing next to my bed. "Mommy, it's time to get up. The clock says 6," she said quietly.

"No, honey is says 2," I corrected her after I squinted at the clock. It was 2:07 a.m.

She insisted that it was a six, so we went to take a look. I got to her room and it didn't have a 6 on it. She cried and said, "Mommy, it did have a 6 on it."

I was quickly reminded that there are *lots* of times the clock reads 6: at 2:06, 2:16, 2:26, 2:36, 2:46, 2:56, and that was just that hour. I had only been focused on the first number, but she didn't know any different. She just happened to have slept through the night the first couple of days. I gave her a hug and told her yes it did have a 6 before but now it was gone. I explained that it was the middle of the night, and Mommy would fix her clock in the morning. I carried her around the house in my arms and we looked out the window at the moon and stars. She was getting tired again and I put her back in her bed and she fell back to sleep. When she woke up again, her clock said 6 in the hour spot and it was time to get up.

That day I fixed her clock by covering up her minute digits so she only saw the hour digit. I explained to her I had forgotten there were some extra 6's on her clock we needed to hide so she wouldn't get mixed up again. She was okay with that. She continued to stay in bed until her clock said 6. Her clock was still 30 minutes fast, so she was actually getting up at 5:30, but on the mornings she woke before her clock said 6, she was able to wait. She would sing or talk to herself until she fell back asleep. That's when I realized the difference between the big girl bed and the crib. In her crib, when she would cry at 5:15 a.m., I wouldn't go to her; instead, I would wait and soon she would put herself back to sleep. She had lost that ability with her new freedom of the big girl bed. With her clock, she was going back to relaxing herself and going back to sleep.

Day by day, I moved the clock a few minutes closer to the actual time, keeping her successful *most* of the time. Sometimes she would wake up a little before it said 6 and she would wait in her bed until it said 6. Finally, she was 'trained' to stay in bed, and hopefully, to stay asleep until 6.

Training is not about blind obedience; it is about guiding your child to understand social norms.

Allowing Independence

✦ ✦ ✦

Moving Ashley to a big girl bed was easy. When we purchased a bunk bed, we moved Danielle to the bottom bunk bed, and Ashley, who was then two-and-a-half years old, moved to the double bed Danielle had been sleeping in. We crossed our fingers and hoped we would luck out with Ashley. She loved her new bed and stayed in it at night. Even in the mornings she didn't climb out. She would cry and wait for me to come up to get her. I finally had to teach her how to climb off the bed in the morning and come downstairs. She didn't realize she could get up all by herself!

Danielle loved sleeping in the bottom bunk, but there was this awesome bed just sitting there, lonely, above her. We purposely left the ladder off so the girls couldn't climb up to the top bunk, but one day I found Danielle sitting on the top bunk, guiding little Ashley on how to climb up! Thankfully, Ashley's legs were not long enough. I guess it was time we put the ladder up and let them start climbing, carefully showing them how to climb down (and always saying a silent prayer of safety!).

Ashley didn't like climbing down; she was too scared. If she climbed up, I had to help her down. On the other hand, Danielle had become a pro at climbing up and down. It was time to let Danielle—who was now four—choose where she wanted to sleep. She *loved* the idea of the top bunk and chose to sleep up there, but I don't think I slept at all the first night. Every move she made, I held my breath, waiting for her to fall out of the top bunk bed. (It didn't matter that there was a permanent railing all the around the bed or that she had never fallen out of bed.) I did, in fact, eventually fall asleep, because one minute I was anxiously listening for any sounds of distress from the bunk bed, and the next thing, Danielle's little nose perched at my face as she stood next to my bed.

"Mommy, time to get up," she half-whispered.

She did it!

Slowly, I got more and more comfortable with her sleeping on the top bunk. Danielle wanted Ashley to sleep in the bunk bed under her. Ashley wasn't excited to change, but my parents were about to visit and we needed the double bed for the weekend. We needed new sheets for the bunk bed, so as an incentive, Ashley got to pick them. She picked Barney sheets. That night, with the Barney sheets on the bottom bunk bed, she was excited to sleep there and slept through the night. She loved her new bed!

Not surprisingly, Danielle loved having her sister in the bottom bunk. I was reminded of the closeness between the two girls when one day at naptime, it started storming. I thought the girls were sound asleep since they didn't come downstairs, scared of the cracking thunder. Then there was an exceptionally loud boom, so I went up to check on them. That's when I saw Danielle, huddled next to her little sister in the bottom bunk, both of them sound asleep. I even took a picture without waking them. It melted my heart.

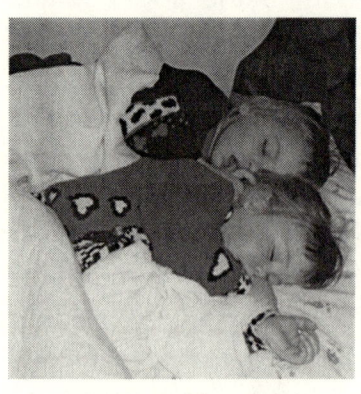

Danielle Keeping Ashley safe

Later, I asked Danielle if Ashley had been scared.

"I thought she might get scared. So I climbed down and gave her a hug," Danielle explained.

✧ ✧ ✧

The day came when Lindsey (who was then two-and-a-half years old) forced me to move her to a big girl bed. I had caught her lying across the top of her crib, trying to figure out how to finish climbing out of it. My stomach dropped, since I knew she would keep trying until she succeeded. It was time to get Lindsey out of the crib before she fell from the top of it and hurt herself. That weekend we had a new bed, and the crib taken down. That was the easy part; the battle had just begun.

Lindsey loved being in a big bed, but only because she loved the freedom it gave her. Really she loved getting out of her big girl bed! I even asked Dan to put her crib back up so I could put her back into the crib, because she kept getting out of her big girl bed. He reminded me of the reason we got the big girl bed for her in the first place: she was already climbing out of the crib, and putting her back in it instead of a big girl bed wouldn't change that. It seemed that no matter what I tried, Lindsey wouldn't settle down to sleep in a big girl bed. It was as if she simply didn't know *how* to settle down . . . then I remembered something!

When Lindsey was about a year old, she had a strange going to sleep pattern. I would put her in her crib, and she would whine a little and settle down. Then, I would hear one loud noise and one loud cry. I would run upstairs; sometimes I would hug her and lay her back down again, and other times, by the time I got there, she was just about asleep. I learned to react slowly to her loud cry. I would walk slowly upstairs to see why she had cried, and many times she would be asleep.

One day, I was putting the girls down for a nap and I had a couple of things to do in my bedroom so I was upstairs a little longer than normal. As I started to walk back downstairs, I glanced into Lindsey's bedroom; the door was open a few inches. I saw her walking around in her crib with her blanket in her hand. I wondered what she was doing, so I waited a few minutes as I stood in the hallway, and then glanced in again. Now she was standing there, leaning on the railing of her crib with her thumb in her mouth. Suddenly, she fell down. I jumped, she cried out, but as I stood still, I watched as Lindsey closed her eyes again and fell asleep. She had actually fallen asleep standing up in her crib, then she fell down, which woke her up! She would cry, but she was now ready to go to sleep. I would never have believed it if I had not seen it with my own eyes! She didn't want to stop and sleep so she kept moving as long as she could until she literally dropped.

Lindsey had learned to fall asleep standing up and now was in a bed without a railing to sleep against. She hadn't learned how to lie down, relax, and fall asleep. She would walk around to get tired like she did in her crib, only now she was able to get out of bed and come downstairs. I would put her back to bed and she would do it over and over again. Finally, she would fall asleep, but this was quickly becoming a routine, and was not one I enjoyed. I would try to lay with her, but she would tell me to leave. Then I would leave, and out she would come. She was winning this game.

The same thing was happening during nap time every day. I would put all three girls down for a nap at the same time every afternoon. This was a sacred time of day for me; an hour of peace and quiet. I would hear them reading a book to their stuffed animals or singing. Soon it would be quiet and they were asleep, but once Lindsey moved to her big girl bed, my sacred time was becoming game time. I would hear her get out of her bed and play with toys, so I would head back upstairs. As soon as Lindsey heard me, she'd run back to her bed and jump in. Another game had started that she was winning.

One day during nap time, I was talking to another stay at home mom on the phone. I looked up to see Lindsey, but I just ignored her as I continued to talk to my friend. Lindsey cuddled up on the couch with me. I just kept talking and she was asleep next to me in a matter of minutes. After my conversation, I carried her upstairs and she finished her nap. The next day, I reminded myself that nap time was also a time for *me* to have peace and quiet, so when Lindsey came down the stairs, I didn't talk to her. I didn't move. She came over to me and I picked her up and held her. She

A Mommy's Road

quickly fell asleep and I carried her upstairs. (Perhaps I didn't really mind since she was my youngest and holding little girls was quickly becoming a thing of the past.) Now I figured the nap time game was a tie; she was falling asleep without a battle, but it was still not in her bed.

One day when she didn't come down, I went upstairs to see if she had actually learned to fall asleep in her bed for nap time. When I peeked into her room, she was sitting on the floor in front of her bookcase, looking at all of the books. The goal was quiet time, and she didn't notice me, so I left. Later when I peeked in, she was back in her big girl bed, sound asleep. The next day, she was working on a puzzle that was on her bookshelf. Some of these puzzles were her sisters' and were much too difficult for her, but she would try them. I was amazed that she would work on a puzzle that was much too advanced for her, but she never yelled out of frustration; she knew she was supposed to be quiet and go to sleep. She would work on the puzzles for awhile, then get tired and climb back into her big girl bed and take her nap. Finally, I had won the nap time game, but she was still winning the bedtime game!

Every night I would tuck her in and carry her back to bed at least two times before she would finally fall asleep. One night, she walked out of her bedroom, peeking through mostly-closed eyes. When I told her to head back to bed, she said, "I *am* sleeping."

I looked over at her and sure enough, her eyes were closed, her thumb was in her mouth, and she was pretending to sleep. I waited and watched as she peeked through her eyes again and walked toward Dan. Just when he turned to notice her, I said, "Shhh, she is sleeping, it looks like we will have to carry her back to bed."

Dan carried her upstairs and she stayed there and fell asleep. We laughed about her idea that she was asleep because she couldn't see us, but we knew we had to find a better solution to this game. She had to learn to go to sleep on her own, somehow, so back to the parenting books I went. They said to put your child to bed at the same time every night, have a consistent bedtime routine, kiss them good night and leave . . . we already did all that. The only thing the books said that we didn't do was close the door to keep the child in their room. That next night after her bedtime routine, I walked out, closed her door and waited.

I could hear her walking around her room, and then she came to her door. She tried to open it, but she couldn't with her little hands. She banged on the door and started yelling. The books told me that no matter how much she yelled or screamed or cried, that I shouldn't give in. The books said that over time, she would get tired and give up. As I heard her kicking the door with her feet and crying and screaming, I was reminded of one important thing: those books didn't know my Lindsey. Once she wanted something she didn't stop, no matter what; and what's more, there were two other girls going to sleep at the same time. They had excellent going to bed and sleep routines, and I was not about to teach them differently. Keeping this all in mind, I opened the door, gave Lindsey a hug, and put her back to bed. I told her I would leave the door open, and she stopped crying and nodded. I went downstairs and waited, and just as I predicted, a few minutes later, she was back downstairs. I carried her upstairs again and put her back into her bed. She was still winning this game.

The very next night, I went against all of the parenting books advice. I stayed in bed with Lindsey after I finished reading her bedtime book. She wanted me to leave, but I told her I was worried about her sleepwalking. I told her about how the other night she had walked in her sleep and I didn't want her to fall down the stairs when she was walking with her eyes closed; I stayed to keep her safe. It wasn't long before she was asleep. Each night, I would stay in bed with her and she (thankfully) would fall asleep. The game was now a tie. Team Mom and Dad hadn't won, but Lindsey was finally falling asleep in her bed, just not alone yet.

After a couple of weeks, it was time for me to start moving out of her bed. I knew the books wanted me to do it cold turkey– just leave her and let her cry and she would eventually learn. But I knew how Lindsey would react and that she could out-will me. I needed to work myself out of staying in her bed with her, *slowly*.

> *Don't be afraid to do what is right for your child, even if it goes against 'expert' advice.*

Allowing Independence

I started by sitting on the floor next to her bed. Each night, I moved a few inches farther away from Lindsey. I was glad when I was getting close to the door, because the light from the hallway allowed me to read my own book while I waited for her to fall asleep. Finally, I was able to kiss her good night and sit just outside of her room. When I heard Lindsey get out of bed, I didn't say anything or even look at her. As soon as she saw me, she turned, climbed back into bed, and settled down to go to sleep. I didn't move a muscle.

I continued to migrate a little more each night across the landing, eventually to the steps. A couple of times, Lindsey came to the edge of her bedroom door and would peek out to see if I was sitting there. I would pretend I hadn't heard her and just kept reading my book.

Eventually, I was able to kiss her good night, walk out her door and quietly sneak down the steps. Once in a while she would get up and come find me, but I would just pick her up without talking or even hugging her and put her back to bed—I gave no positive *or* negative reaction . . . I simply put her back into bed. Then I would wait on the top step for a few minutes so a new game wouldn't start, but she never came out to me twice. She might have peeked, but if she did, I was there, so she went back to bed. I was winning; she was finally able to fall asleep in her big girl bed all by herself.

Just as the parenting books had predicted, *'if you lay with your child when they go to sleep, when they wake up in the middle of the night, they need you to be able to go back to sleep,'* and it wasn't long before Lindsey started appearing next to my bed in the middle of the night. At first, I just pulled her into bed with us and let her sleep there, but that got old, fast. Even though she was little, she always took up my part of the bed, and I couldn't sleep well.

This time, the parenting books did give me a good solution: Lindsey had a choice. I could take her back to bed, or she could lay on the floor next to our bed. I put a spare pillow and blanket next to my side of the bed so I was ready for her. Of course, her first choice was to sleep in our bed and I said that was not one of the options. Of her two options, she picked the floor. I didn't give her much attention; I just pointed at the pillow and soon she was asleep on the floor. Once she was asleep, one of us would carry her back upstairs. If she picked go back to bed, I would carry her upstairs and put her into bed, but always giving her very little attention. Once in awhile she would change her mind after I made her lay on the floor; she would stand up and say, "Now, I want to go back to bed."

I knew this battle was over when Dan got up one morning and noticed Lindsey was on the floor next to our bed. He mentioned he didn't hear her come in or hear me talking to her. I told him she didn't come down last night. He pointed to her. She had come in, laid down next to our bed on the floor, and fallen asleep there all on her own. The game was over and we had *both* won.

Stop Nagging

Getting ready in the morning had begun to get easier now that the girls were preschoolers and were becoming more physically independent. They could dress themselves with little help from me. I quickly discovered I was still busy with them, but it was only verbally; I spent a great deal of effort reminding them: "Did you brush your teeth? Don't forget to brush your hair."

To complicate things, I couldn't remember who I had reminded to do what. Many times, the girls would get frustrated with me because I had already asked them. They also each moved in their own direction and at their own speeds; it was no longer a smooth assembly line like it was when I was in control. It was time to re-gain some of that control, so I had everyone get ready at the same time, doing the same things.

. . . But that was a disaster. Each of them took a different length of time to get their clothes on. Ashley would just do it and be done. Danielle would sing and look at the mirror every step of the way. Lindsey would start to get dressed, stop to play, and then go back to dressing. I stuck with my plan and made Ashley wait for her sisters. Then they all went into the bathroom to brush their teeth. Before I could turn around, I heard yelling and falling. As I asked what happened, they all talked at once about the stools. I had three girls in the bathroom brushing their teeth with two sinks and two step stools. What did I *think* would happen?

Later that day, I started to realize I needed to look ahead, not backwards. I couldn't return to the way things were; the girls had grown independent and I needed to encourage that, not try to take back control. So I started to think of the original problem: it was that I was doing too much asking and reminding. It wasn't that they couldn't do it, but rather, it was that I felt like they couldn't remember to do everything. That's when I decided to make a chart: The Get Ready Chart.

I wrote down the list of things that I was reminding them of every day. Danielle could read, Lindsey couldn't, and Ashley was somewhere in-between, so I wrote the list

Danielle, Lindsey, and Ashley ALL getting ready

and drew pictures of each task. I put the chart on the bathroom door and I waited for them to see it and ask, "What's this, Mommy?"

I gathered all three girls together and said, "Let's read it together." I had Danielle read the title, "The Get Ready Chart."

I explained they would read the chart each morning to be sure they were ready for their day. The girls took turns *'reading'* the tasks and we talked about what each one meant. They were all very excited.

The next morning, each girl ran upstairs to The Get Ready Chart and I heard them reading the chart at their own speed and in their own order. When they were done, I only had to ask if they finished their chart.

Of course, it didn't take long before they stopped

Allowing Independence

reading the chart and wouldn't do something, but whenever I noticed, I would take that child by the hand to the chart, and together, we read it like a check list. They would see the thing they forgot and run off to do it. I realized I was teaching them to get ready on their own without me checking. They were becoming more independent and not just obedient.

With The Get Ready Chart actually working, I started to wonder, *"When was I just demanding them to be obedient?"* Then it occurred to me: after every meal.

> *Being obedient is not independence.*
> *Independence is your child doing things*
> *on their own without being told.*

It had all started years earlier when Danielle, who was four, and Ashley, three, were able to sit in chairs without their booster seats. After they finished eating, each girl had to take their dishes off the table and put them on the counter by the dishwasher. At first they enjoyed doing it; they felt like big kids. Lindsey wanted to do what her sisters were doing before she was out of her booster chair, and she couldn't even reach the counter, but I would get her out of her booster seat and let her carry her plate from the table to me as I stood by the dishwasher. There were many spills that happened between the table and the counter, but she was learning. She was so proud she was able to do it like her big sisters. (Actually, Dan had to constantly encourage me to be patient with the messes and point out the bigger picture of her learning.)

As the girls all got more proficient at placing their dishes in the sink, we shifted so they had to start putting their dirty dishes *into* the dishwasher. They were also at the age where they knew this was a job and it was *not* fun. Many nights as they would set their dishes on the counter and start to walk away, I had to remind them to put their dishes in the dishwasher, and they would obey and do it. I started to force myself to be quiet and wait to see what they would do. Many times they would leave their dishes on the counter. I would wait until I was done eating and was clearing off the table, and then I would shout for them to return to put their dishes into the dishwasher.

"But I am already ALL the way upstairs," one of them would cry.

"Sorry about that. But it's your job so come back down and do it," I would explain.

It wasn't long before they would remember to do it, but they did it because they didn't want to make a special trip down the stairs. Now I was teaching them to be responsible and not just obedient.

This worked out really well at night, but occasionally in the morning, we would get busy and all of us were in a hurry. That's when I would find myself falling back to doing it myself because it was easier. One day I had a very busy morning, and I ended up leaving the house to get the younger girls to preschool without going back into the kitchen. We ended up not getting back to the house until the middle of the afternoon and when

I finally walked into the kitchen, I saw Danielle's bowl of leftover cereal and milk from breakfast, thickening in its bowl on the kitchen table. As I reached to grab it, I realized that in just a couple of hours, Danielle would be home to see *her* mess. I lingered on how gross it was, and I put the bowl back on the table. I walked out of the kitchen and didn't go back in so I wouldn't be tempted to dump the gross mess.

This idea wasn't borne out of my own brain; I got the idea of natural consequences from one of my parenting books. The most important concept about natural consequences was that I had to bite my tongue. If the child thought about or realized it (whatever "it" was) all on their own, they would remember and it wasn't a game.

When Danielle returned home from school, she grabbed her snack and headed to the table. "Ick, Mom, the table is a mess," she yelled.

I calmly walked into the kitchen and explained to her, "It's your cereal bowl from this morning."

She looked at me with very sad eyes and explained she was sorry. I told her that it was fine, but she needed to take care of her dishes because it was her job. She complained the entire time about how gross it was and how much it smelled . . . but she took care of it. From that day forward, she always remembered to grab her dishes and put them in the dishwasher.

Natural consequences work!

Of course there were times when someone else forgot, but as long as I remembered not to pick up after them, they would learn. I discovered and reinforced the importance of natural consequences.

Staying Home Alone

The first time I really thought I was teaching my children to be independent was when they were old enough to be left at home for a few minutes. That was a big step, and they demanded it *way* before I was ready for it.

When Danielle was only nine years old, she hated having to stop what she was doing just to get in the car for ten minutes to run her sister to dance class and then come back home. There were many times I would see the older two just sitting and watching TV and knew they wouldn't move for the next 30 minutes, never mind the ten minutes I would be gone. I started thinking about it. I talked it over with Dan and he agreed they were getting old enough, and he liked the idea of starting with a very short time.

Basically, I asked myself what could possibly happen in ten minutes? Not a question to think about before I went to sleep. I dreamt of a house fire and the girls' home alone. Of course I was arrested for neglect for leaving my little girls home alone. I woke up to my mug shot appearing on TV, looking like a drugged mom since I had been crying for hours.

Needless to say, it took me a few more weeks before I could forget my dream and actually leave them home alone. I trained them on all the safety issues. Of course they knew how to use the house phone (this was before cell phones) and could easily call our family friend, Sandy, who lived five minutes away, or even walk down to Toni's house, which was two houses away. They knew about 911, and I kept reminding myself that eight-year-old Ashley would follow every rule, and Danielle would make sure they both were happy. The only one that wasn't ready to be left home alone was Lindsey, who was six, but I was taking her with me. We had practiced what to say on the phone if someone called and I wasn't home. They were to say, "She can't come to the phone right now." (That line was memorized after they told people I was in the bathroom or shower.)

The first day I left them, all I could think about was the house catching fire, so I started to hurry out of the driveway with Lindsey in the car. Then I realized the more likely thing to happen would be a fender bender if I was rushing and I would be held up for a couple of hours. If that happened, there would be no way to tell the kids, since cell phones weren't common, so I slowed down and drove like an elderly person. Lindsey loved being the only one in the car and started talking about being the only child. She wondered if we could always go without her sisters. I told her, "Let's take it one day at a time."

When I got home, everything was just fine. Danielle and Ashley were still sitting on the couch watching the same show as when I left. I had to yell to get them to notice I was even back. It was no big deal to them, but a life changer for me.

Each week, everything went along just fine. I was even leaving them playing or reading without the TV on. They hardly noticed when I wasn't there. I was still gone just ten minutes, but I was beginning to think I might be able to stop and grab milk from the grocery store soon and be gone for up to 30 minutes.

> *It is usually two steps forward, then a step back. Remember that you are still moving forward!*

One day, the girls were outside in our front yard playing with the neighbor girl, Maria (not her real name). I called Lindsey in to tell her to get ready for dance class and I warned the older girls they would be coming inside in a few minutes. The time came, I called the girls inside, and they protested that they wanted to just play outside while I was gone. I told them no; they had to be inside, and I told Maria she had to head home.

Danielle and Ashley went inside, Maria walked toward her house, and Lindsey and I started on our way. But, as I drove down the street, I remembered hearing Maria saying, "You get to stay home alone?"

I looked in the rearview mirror to see Maria heading back toward our house and I realized this could be a problem, so I drove around the block. The girls were instructed NOT to open the door to anyone. But as I circled the block, I saw Maria walking into our house. I pulled back into the driveway and walked up to the front door, just in time to hear Maria shout, "You get to stay home alone!"

Allowing Independence

I told her to go back to her house in a tone that should have told her not to argue, but she started to anyway. Beside myself, I growled at Ashley and Danielle: "Get into the car now! You can't be trusted."

The phrase *'can't be trusted'* was actually what I wanted to say to Maria, since I had told her to go home. It was a fact that I didn't trust her; I had witnessed her being sneaky before. I didn't say anything to her, but guided her directly out the door. Danielle and Ashley knew my tone and didn't say a word. They ran to join Lindsey in the car. We took Lindsey to dance class, late, and Danielle, Ashley, and I sat on the bench in the dance studio to wait the hour for the class to be finished instead of heading back home. I thought that would be a good start to the punishment.

After a few moments and a couple of deep breaths, I started to think clearly. How do I not make too much of this? I realized I was more upset than I should have been. I was glad we were in public so I was quieter than I would have been in the car or at home. I thought about what really happened instead of just reacting. The girls explained their point of view.

"We knew her," Ashley cried.

I pointed out that they were not supposed to open the door to anyone when they were alone. (When I was home, they were allowed to open the door to people they knew, but not to strangers.) Ashley said she didn't know that. I had just told Danielle because she was the one I was training to be home alone, but I had never told Ashley.

"I know, Mom, but I thought it would be rude NOT to answer the door. She knew we were there," Danielle explained through her tears.

We just sat and waited, and they didn't move off the bench. Ashley didn't know the rule and Danielle didn't want to hurt anyone's feelings. Not a surprise. I started to focus on **why** I was **so** upset. Then I realized it was Maria who I was really mad at. I had told her to go back home, as my girls were going in the house. She was also someone I didn't trust in my house even when I **was** there. She was just that kind of kid. I had never told my daughters that; I couldn't. They had let in a *'friend'* and I thought of it as danger. That was the big difference. By the end of Lindsey's dance class, I had the perfect punishment in mind: an apology to someone they respected and someone who *wasn't* me or Dan: Ms. Jennifer, their dance teacher. Danielle and Ashley apologized to Ms. Jennifer for making Lindsey late. Being a mom, I hoped she would handle it right without an explanation. She saw they had been crying and said the perfect response, "Whatever you did to make her late, I am sure you will never do again."

"No, we won't," they said in unison.

It wasn't until the next week when I took Lindsey to dance that I got a chance to tell Ms. Jennifer the whole story. Not only did I leave Danielle and Ashley home alone again, but it was an extra ten-minute trip this time. This episode was a lesson that had helped Ashley and Danielle to be more responsible at home.

In the Rearview Mirror of Allowing Independence

Looking back, I appreciate the importance to teaching the girls honesty, but I have to admit I was not a good example. I told my share of little white lies, as it was just easier than facing temper tantrums. When the girls wanted more juice, I had an empty pitcher in the refrigerator that I took out and said, 'All gone. We will have to get some from the store.' They were totally fine with that. The next day, I took out the full pitcher. I felt I was justified to save a temper tantrum with just a little white lie. At first I felt guilty training Danielle to stay in bed until her clock said a certain time, but at the time, I really just needed my sleep. Afterwards, I realized I taught her how to comfort herself back to sleep or entertain herself until it was time to get up. The reason I did it was selfish, but in the end it was for a better outcome.

Once I discovered how successful natural consequences were, I tried to use them as much as possible. Natural consequences are how adults learn things in life. The key I struggled with was to keep my mouth shut and let the girls learn their own lessons. Not to say, 'Now you will remember, won't you,' or 'I bet you learned your lesson.' If I did, it negated the lesson and they were just being lectured at. As long as I could keep my mouth shut, the lesson was learned.

Staying home alone was the first time I thought I was teaching independence, but doing their own self-care without nagging reminders were the steps that lead up to that big action. I heard once that when you have little kids, you are physically exhausted from carrying them around and helping them with things. As they grow and become more independent, the exhaustion shifts from physical to emotional exhaustion—and it is all from worry!

Chapter 10:
Delegating Decisions

As a busy mom, I found I was fighting the same battles over and over again. That just drove me crazy. I would try to think of a fast solution to a problem, and many times that solution was actually a choice I was asking the girls to make. I was just trying to stop the repeat behavior, but what I was actually doing was giving them options and teaching decision-making skills.

All Done

I never liked the high chair pickup game that every child plays. The girl in the high chair throws her cup on the floor; I would pick it up and go back to eating. Soon the spoon is on the floor, and I would pick it up. I think with just one child, you just play the game without much thought of it. But as I was starting the second round of this game with Ashley, it got on my nerves, fast. One night as I was picking up her cup, Ashley threw her spoon down and it hit me in the head. "That's it, all done," I announced.

    I cleaned up Ashley and got her out of the high chair. I began to question my decision, as Ashley now wanted to go back in the high chair and cried like she was starving to death. I didn't want to start a new game of *in the high chair, out of the high chair*. But would my toddler starve to death?

Luckily when this happened, we were almost done eating, so we finished and cleaned up the table. I decided I better do a little research in my parenting books on toddlers starving to death. (Yes, I may have overreacted.) I discovered that kids actually know what their bodies need to eat. Some meals they didn't eat much, but would make up for it at the next meal. Some children would actually eat only a few bites of protein one meal and the next day eat several servings. The book stated, *'A parent usually gets in the way of their child's normal eating behavior by trying to control their foods within each meal.'*

With this new knowledge, I was confident Ashley was actually trying to tell me something with this pick-up game. I watched during the next meal, and as Ashley started to eat, she was not throwing her tools on the floor. The first things to head to the floor were certain foods. I watched as she was selecting what she was done eating: no more bananas, as they were all headed to the floor . . . and I just watched. Then she started banging her spoon on the tray. I looked around to discover there was no more ham on her tray, so I gave her a few more chucks of ham. She grabbed them and ate them as she stopped banging her spoon. In the past, I would have held her spoon or taken it away; I never realized she was trying to tell me something. I continued to watch as she finally threw her spoon on the floor. I didn't pick it up; I just watched. Ashley grabbed her sippy cup to drink her milk. Then she picked up a few more peas. As I glanced away, I heard her sippy cup head to the floor. Again, I didn't pick it up. I waited and watched. Then she started to wipe her hands all over her tray and try to push everything off. I had never seen this behavior before, but decided she was done, so I cleaned her up as I announced, "All done."

This time, I set Ashley down next to her toys in the next room where we could watch her as we finished eating. She played with no crying or demanding that she wanted to go back into her chair.

I was amazed by what I just witnessed. I wasn't sure I believed the parenting books about a toddler knowing what their body needed to eat, and I wasn't quite convinced this wasn't just a good night at the table. So I continued to watch and learn as Ashley was trying to communicate her needs. When she would hit her spoon on her tray, I would survey her tray to determine what food she was missing. I would then ask her, "More ham?" (or whatever else was missing from her tray).

She wasn't old enough to talk yet, but I knew when she did learn to talk, a simple word like, 'more' would be easy for her to learn. I was looking ahead to the day that spoon banging could stop!

I started to realize that sometimes she threw her sippy cup because it was empty. Many times she pushed it across her tray, but sometimes it fell over the side. I started to pick up her cup to see if it was empty. If it was, I would pour in some more milk and say, "More milk?"

If it wasn't empty, I would just keep it. A similar thing

would happen with her spoon. Sometimes Ashley would throw her spoon to the floor, but then reach over the side and cry. I would give it back, but only once. If she did it again, no more spoon for the night. She learned to keep what she wanted.

It didn't take long before Ashley would just push all of her food to the outsides of her tray instead of throwing her spoon and cup to the floor. It was kind of like she was wiping her tray off with her hands. I would clean her up and "All done," as I set her on the floor.

Of course there were nights Ashley was not done eating, but was just having a hard time sitting in her highchair. But when she played the pickup game and all her tools were on the floor, she was all done; she didn't get to go back into her highchair, no matter how hard she cried. Sometimes we finished eating quickly to clean up the table, since listening to a toddler cry is not a pleasant experience. But we never put her back her highchair.

I was shocked that the pickup game was actually a communication technique . . . I had just missed the message. Even as a toddler, she was making a decision of what she wanted to eat more of and when she was done eating.

> *Be sure you are 'listening' to your child so eating doesn't become a power struggle.*

As I continued to spend my meals watching what was happening instead of just reacting, I witnessed something else. Two-year-old Danielle would ask, "More peas?"

Dan would say, "Eat up your ham first." When she would finish her ham, he would give her more peas. But as we cleared the table, I noticed she didn't eat them. I was confused. So the next day at lunch when she asked me for more applesauce, I decided to give her some even though she hadn't eaten anything else on her plate. She ate up the applesauce, and then moved on to the rest of her food. But for the first time, I saw her eat all of her turkey next, then her beans. I was still puzzled, but I was looking for the clues.

That night, I watched again as Danielle ate one food at a time. Once she would start her next food, she never went back to the previous one. After I watched her finish her favorite food and move on to the next one, I asked if she wanted more of her favorite food. She said, "No."

Since she had started the next food, she was done. I started to remember that even when she was a baby, she would get mad when I would switch between baby food fruits and vegetables. She would stop eating her fruit when I would give her a vegetable and would make a face when I switched back. I was shocked to realize she was making decisions about her food even as a baby, but I hadn't been listening.

Lindsey demonstrated her decision-making skills when she was finished eating, just like Ashley did with the pickup game. She was very content to sit in her highchair a long time. I think it was because she was a good eater and liked to be where the action was. She didn't like to be taken out of her highchair early and be left out. Whenever we pulled her out of her highchair, we said, "Up."

It wasn't long before she was lifting her hands above her head as if to say, "Up."

We would clean her up and set her down to play until the rest of us were done. One day she said, 'up' in front of a friend, who pointed out that she was saying 'up' for down. I was confused, since we had to lift her up out of the highchair to get her out. But my friend pointed out she was actually getting down, so I was confusing our poor child. I am sure it wasn't the only time!

Wear That!

Getting ready for the day was a process that went smoothly *most* of the time. Through trial and error, I found that how my day began would set the tone for the rest of the day. When getting everyone ready to go in the morning went smoothly, the day would be calm and relaxing. However, when the morning started out with frustration, the day seemed to drag on, exacerbating my impatience. So I kept it as simple as possible.

One way that I did that was that I put clothes together to be worn as a set, for example, the Barney shirt was always worn with a pair of matching purple shorts. Many times, that meant purple socks, but it didn't matter that many shirts would match the purple shorts. The Barney shirt was always worn with the purple shorts. I actually folded each pair of shorts and pants with a certain shirt to make a set. (Before you judge me, remember I had three little girls with clothes of very similar size. And I could remember who had which T-shirt, but the pants and shorts would often look identical.)

There were days when an accident would happen, but I only changed what was needed. If someone spilled on their shirt during lunch, we would put on a clean one. Each girl had a stack of random shirts for that. But if their pants needed to be changed, I often changed their entire outfit. (Yes, I hate to admit it, but I did.)

My smooth morning routine started with Danielle. She was always the first one up each day. As I grabbed her outfit, I was mentally preparing what the other girls would be wearing. As I put the Barney T-shirt over Danielle's head, I knew that Ashley would be wearing her Baby Bop T-shirt. Lindsey was still in sleepers, so she would wear a purple one that day. Nice and simple and easy. But it didn't last long.

Danielle would peek over the top of her drawer to see the pile of her clothes and say, "Wear that!"

Many times, she would help herself and start pulling clothes out of the drawer, making a mess of my folded sets of clothes. That led to the frustration that caused the day to become a long, impatient one. I have to admit that the first several weeks of this, I tried as many tactics as possible so I could still get my way in peace. I would pull out her outfit when she wasn't looking, or a little distraction worked great. The days that didn't work, I would just play the 'I'm bigger than you, I am the mom, do as I say' card. She responded with her pre two-year-old temper tantrum. That led to a long day of anger and more temper tantrums. It was time for me to figure out a way to let go.

> *Let go of control! You are bigger than your child now, but someday they may be bigger than you.*

At first it was a disaster as I let her look into the drawer. Danielle would pull out what she wanted as she announced, "Wear that!"

In the process of pulling out one of the top outfits, she would mess up the outfit under it and next to it. Other mornings she wanted to look at everything in the drawer. By the time she figured out what she wanted, Lindsey was waking up crying, and Ashley was taking off her own clothes. By the time I got back to Danielle, she had completely emptied her drawer of clothes. She was standing there, holding up her purple shorts and a pink striped top, proudly saying, "Wear that!"

I now had an entire drawer of clothes to refold into sets and what she wanted to wear didn't even match! Once again I played the 'I'm bigger than you, I am the mom, do as I say' card. She responded with her now two-year-old temper tantrum, which again led to a long day of anger and many more temper tantrums. I needed to have some of the control back.

I realized that not only was I frustrated, but Danielle was getting overwhelmed with all of her options, too. I started pulling out just two choices. "Do you want to wear purple Barney today or pink stripes?"

She quickly picked the pink stripes. I didn't even

give her a choice of shorts. The pink shorts go with the pink striped shirt. But I let her pick white socks or pink socks. She was very happy that she got to pick two times. She didn't care she didn't have a drawer full of options. Finally, I realized she just wanted to pick what she would wear.

For a few months, I was able to put Ashley in a similar outfit based on what Danielle had picked, but it wasn't long before Ashley was starting to pull her clothes out of her drawer while I was putting on Danielle's socks. But this time, I was ready, so I quickly changed my morning routine. As soon as Danielle would pick out her outfit, I would put the one she didn't want away and pull out two options for Ashley. Danielle was already starting the 'Me Do It' stage, so I was able to switch focus between the girls. It really didn't matter to me if the girls wore similar outfits; it was just easier. Ashley was very happy to have a choice of one of two outfits. And I felt no loss of control this time. Danielle was able to work on getting her own clothes on as I got Ashley dressed. The mornings were still going smoothly.

But as you might imagine, things never stayed the same for long. Danielle had found her dresses hanging in the closet. So as I would pull out her two outfits, she would open the closet door to wear a dress. I would ask which outfit of the two she wanted to wear, but she would be pointing to a dress and say, "No, wear that!"

I didn't think a morning at the park was a good day to wear her Easter dress. So, I played the 'I'm bigger than you, I am the mom, do as I say' card. She responded with her now three-year-old temper tantrum, which led to a long day of anger and many more temper tantrums. So I explained that the days we stayed home she could wear her Easter dress, but not at the park. It didn't take me long to realize she wanted to have more options than two. And she was always going to pick a dress!

I went shopping for some casual-type dresses. What I found were some longer tops that I could put knit pants under (which are now called leggings). I hung the knit pants on a hanger under its matching longer top and put the set in her closet. Now Danielle's options were: the two outfits I had pulled from her drawer or something from her closet. She would usually point to something in her closet and say, "Wear that!"

Danielle loves dresses

When I pulled down the hanger, she would have a long top and a pair of matching knit pants to wear. She was thrilled, and I was happy.

Ashley didn't seem to focus on the "Wear that!" stage. Either she wasn't concerned about clothes, or I had learned all of the hard lessons with Danielle. More than likely, she was just very content with the routine of the morning and what she put on just didn't matter.

Lindsey, on the other hand, was able to find a way to demand her own independence. She would say,

Delegating Decisions

"Wear that *and* that!"

She would pick a shirt from one set, but pick the shorts from the other set! She wasn't willing to pick one complete outfit. Sometimes I was able to outsmart her with two similar colored outfits, so it didn't matter. But when that wasn't possible, my first reaction was the 'I'm bigger than you, I am the mom, do as I say' card. She responded with her pre two-year-old temper tantrum, which led to a long day of anger and many more temper tantrums.

I was reminded that just because something worked for the other two girls, didn't mean it would work with Lindsey. My first approach was to distract her with the choice of socks. As soon as she selected the blue cow top, for example, I would quickly open the sock drawer to give her a choice of white or blue socks. As I laid out her two sock options, I quickly put on her blue shorts. That worked for a day, and then she was ready for me. As soon as I opened up the sock drawer, she swiftly reached in and grabbed a pair. She was going to wear the pink socks with the purple shorts! I realized I was the one with a choice now. Would I play the 'I'm bigger than you, I am the mom, do as I say' card, and have her respond with her now two-year-old temper tantrum? Or should I let her wear pink socks with her purple shorts? I will admit that it took me a minute to decide which to choose, but I let it go when I realized we weren't going anywhere that day.

Several weeks later, we were at the park with the playgroup. One of the other moms said to me, "You let

Lindsey pick her own socks?"

I had no idea what she was talking about until I looked at Lindsey. She was wearing a Barney T-shirt, purple shorts and pink socks. I smiled and said, "Yes, she is so proud to pick out her own socks."

The mom shook her head and said, "I could never do that."

I smiled as I watched my independent Lindsey proudly wear her pink socks. I realized <u>I had</u> grown up alongside my children as we had moved through the 'Wear that!' stage.

> *As adults, we sometimes have more to learn than our children.*

✧ ✧ ✧

In the blink of an eye, the girls were now pre-teens and starting to shop in the Juniors section of stores. I was entirely unprepared for what I saw there. Just because Danielle had outgrown the children sizes didn't mean she was ready for young adult styles. I was in shock; and she was beyond excited. Quickly, I found myself using phases I thought I would never say, like, "You are never wearing that!" Or, "I don't care if that is what everyone is wearing; my daughter is NOT going to be wearing it."

"So what am I going to wear? Am I am stuck wearing mommy clothes? Do you get to decide what I wear forever?" asked Danielle.

Even though my first thought was, *'yes,'* I quickly realized we were in another decision-making stage. It was her decision, but I wasn't about to let her wear some of the styles that were in that section. We took a break for lunch, and for me to calm down. With a better attitude, I told her I would try to keep my opinions to myself as she pointed to the different styles she liked. After she had pointed out several styles, I told her which couple she could not try on. I let her try one outfit I still wasn't happy with, but after she saw herself in it, she didn't like it either. Danielle was able to find something she liked and I felt was appropriate. However, this was just the beginning of the struggle for appropriate clothes.

By the time the other girls were moving into the Juniors section, I had learned my lesson from Danielle. I let them pick out and try on any clothes they wanted. I waited to hear their reactions to the outfits, and many times they didn't like the things I would deem inappropriate, so it wasn't a battle anyway. It was much less stressful to only talk about the outfits they liked instead of the whole section of clothes. After many battles over inappropriate clothes, my final answer was, "I will not pay for that."

> *Teenage behaviors sometimes mimic toddler behavior.*

I decided I couldn't dictate what they wore, though I am sure they would say I did. But what I could do was decide what I was willing to spend money on. Most of the time they didn't want to use their own money for clothes, so they didn't get what I deemed inappropriate!

Friend Time

At first, the girls' friends were the children of Dan and my friends. Danielle's first friends, Laura, Andrew, and Marie, were in our first playgroup. Ashley's first friends, Matthew and Katelyn, were their siblings. After we moved to Arizona, the girls' friends were once again from the playgroup we joined.

Danielle made friends at school, but really just played with them there. We didn't connect with them outside of school; perhaps we were just too busy. When Ashley started preschool, she made a new friend, Ashleigh. They loved playing together at preschool and it wasn't long before Ashley started asking if she could play at Ashleigh's house. I quickly informed her that she couldn't just invite herself over (even though that is just what kids do). But I knew it wouldn't be long before Ashley would ask her to come over to play at our house. I had only talked to Ashleigh's mom briefly coming and going at preschool, so I decided it was time to get to know Ashleigh and her mom better. I scheduled a play date with Ashleigh and her mom. I explained it would be good to see how the girls got along together outside of school. Actually, we were both checking each other out to see if we could trust each other with our precious child. Ashleigh's mom felt the same way, so we even met again at her house so I could feel more comfortable. After we both passed inspection, the kids started having play dates for a few hours. It was great watching the girls play with kids their own age.

It was a huge adjustment for Lindsey to understand

why only Ashley had her own special friend over to play. All the other times we had friends over, the kids were all friends with each other. But, this time it was different. This was Ashley's friend and Lindsey was told to let Ashley play with her friend alone, but Lindsey felt completely left out.

> *Even preschoolers want to pick their own friends. But they are still young enough for you to approve their choices.*

I explained to Lindsey, "Ashley is older and goes to preschool. Next year you will go to preschool and make new friends, too."

"What about Danielle? She has no special friends," Lindsey pointed out. I told her Danielle had friends at kindergarten and Danielle proceeded to tell Lindsey their names. I was glad Lindsey didn't ask why they hadn't come to our house to play. (Danielle was not as social, and at this point, kindergarten was enough time with friends for her.) But Lindsey still wanted her own special friend; she didn't like being left out from what her sisters could do.

After waking up from a nap the next afternoon, Lindsey had an imaginary friend. Her name was Ashleigh Kibbe, the exact same name as Ashley's preschool friend. Instead of challenging her on it, I just went along with it and gave Ashleigh Kibbe an extra snack (which Lindsey ate). Ashleigh Kibbe sat at the supper table with a plate and fork, but no extra food was given to her.

I was very happy that both Ashley and Danielle went along with it. I told them Lindsey had an imaginary friend visiting today. The next morning, Lindsey's Ashleigh Kibbe came back to have some breakfast. As Dan walked into the kitchen to say goodbye to Lindsey, he sat down on the chair and Lindsey started screaming. I just pulled him up off the chair, and talked to the chair to see if make-believe Ashleigh Kibbe was okay. That calmed Lindsey down, so then I introduced a very confused Dan to Ashleigh Kibbe, also known as the empty chair. He had no idea what had happened and who this was, but he had learned to just go with the flow. He asked Lindsey all about her imaginary friend and acted like we had a friend visiting. As he said goodbye to the girls, he included Lindsey's Ashleigh Kibbe. I walked him out to tell him it had just started yesterday and I had forgotten to tell him since he worked late the night before. "No problem," he turned to me. "I wonder how long this will last?" he mused.

Lindsey's imaginary friend, Ashleigh Kibbe, continued to appear off and on for a while, and seemed to pop up at interesting times. One day I finally got the three girls back in the car after playing at the park. I had just headed down the road when Lindsey yelled, "Mom! You forgot Ashleigh Kibbe!"

Well, I wasn't about to go back to the park, so I slowed the car down a little bit and rolled down the window and yelled, "Come on, Ashleigh Kibbe. You can do it, run faster, almost here, just a little bit farther, jump. Did she make it Lindsey?"

"Yup, I got her, thanks Mommy," Lindsey said as she reached over her car seat to buckle the empty seat belt next to her.

"Great job, Ashleigh Kibbe," I replied. The other two girls just smiled. They were having fun with it, too.

When we were in a rental car visiting the grandparents, the girls were fighting over the back seat because they weren't in the minivan, and Lindsey decided there was no place for Ashleigh Kibbe to sit. I pointed out there was one spot up here between Dan and me. She agreed, but then added another imaginary friend, Mike, to the car, so I said, "Mike can sit on the floor by your feet, but just this time."

Lindsey was happy with that and smiled. As I looked back at her, I realized her smile was just like her sisters' smiles. She knew her friends were imaginary; she had just outgrown them. I was right. That was the last time she had her imaginary friend.

✧ ✧ ✧

Neighborhood children became friends with the girls just from them playing outside. It was easy for me to adjust to these new friends because I could be outside and watch them for as long as I wanted. If I felt like everyone got along and I could trust the neighbor kids, I would let myself go inside for a minute. I was gone for five minutes the first time, and built it up from there.

One day when I went back outside to check on them, I couldn't find them. They were not outside playing where I left them. I yelled up and down the street, my chest tightening with fear. When they finally heard me yelling and came running out of our neighbor Maria's (again, not her real name) house, I was mad at them for going inside a stranger's house to play.

I yelled at all three of them. "Get in the house, now!"

In that moment, I knew I was yelling because I was scared when I couldn't find them, and I was mad they had gone into someone's house without asking or without me checking out the house and the parents first. It took me awhile before I really heard what they were telling me. They had gone *through* Maria's house to her backyard to play. There was a fence, so it was easier to run through her house than through the side gate. They didn't understand what they did wrong; they were still outside playing. As I finally understood their logic, I pointed out that with the fence there, I couldn't see them from the street. I couldn't see they were still outside. Finally, I had calmed down and they understood the problem. No one had really done something against the rules . . . we just needed a new rule. And I did apologize for yelling at them, but I also explained that I was scared.

So, with that, we established a new rule: the girls had to come home to ask me if they could walk into someone's house, no matter what; it didn't matter if they were just going through the house to play outside in that friend's backyard. Ashley said, "Just like at the park when we go to another part to play, we have to tell you."

"Exactly," I said. But I felt uncomfortable. I had witnessed Maria and her younger sister playing outside without much supervision. Whenever I did talk to their mom, I felt uncomfortable. She didn't pass my inspection. Now what? I couldn't tell the girls they couldn't play with Maria. We were neighbors. And because I had never been invited, I couldn't have a rule they couldn't walk into Maria's house without me. At first, each time they would ask if they could go to her backyard, I would find excuses: 'It was lunch time,' or, 'Just not today.' Then Ashley asked, "Why can we *never* go into her backyard?"

Luckily, I thought fast. "How about she plays in our backyard?"

> *When you are uncomfortable with your child's friend, keep them close. Observe them interacting with your child and other children so you can adjust (or firm up) your opinion.*

"Cool," Ashley said as she ran and asked the others. They all yelled in excitement and came running. Maria didn't have to go home to tell her mom where she was; she just followed the girls through our house into our backyard and they all went back to playing. I had my ears glued to the backyard, but I stayed out of eyesight. It wasn't long before I heard Maria asking to play inside.

Ashley came in to ask if they could play inside.

Since I knew where this was coming from, I said, "No, while Maria is over you will just play outside today. If you are done playing outside, that's fine, and she can go home."

I couldn't imagine having a friend in my house

playing without her parents knowing where she was. I continued to listen. Soon I heard Maria say, "I want to see your bedrooms."

In a minute, Danielle walked in to ask if she could show Maria her room.

"Not today," I answered, "It's almost time for lunch."

I followed Danielle into the backyard to warn the girls that, in five minutes, Maria would need to head home since it was almost lunchtime. To my utter shock, Maria turned to me and told me she could stay for lunch.

My shock was threefold: firstly, I had not asked her to stay for lunch, and secondly her parents had no idea where she had been for the last 45 minutes. And thirdly, something just felt off about her, and I was beginning not to like this child.

I gathered myself quickly and decided to respond very casually. "Maria, in five minutes you will need to head home. I am sure your mom will have lunch ready, too."

As I watched the clock for the last five minutes of their play time, I realized I was more protective of my girls than Maria's mom was, but that didn't make her mom a poor mother; it was just different. My fundamental problem was just that I really didn't like Maria as a friend for my girls.

During lunch, the girls and I talked about Maria, and I found out that they didn't really have fun with Maria. She wanted to come inside all of the time, *and* she was boring. I found it so interesting that they were getting the same feeling about Maria that I was. The more we talked (and the less I pushed my opinion), I came to find out that they didn't know they could tell Maria no. If she asked them for something, they came to ask me. When they asked me, I assumed they wanted to do it, but that wasn't always the case. After that conversation, going forward when they came to me for permission, I asked them what they wanted to do. Most of the time their answer was, "No, I am having fun out front. I don't want to play in the backyard. Maria just keeps asking."

To help them find the voice to their *no*, I would give them some excuse why they couldn't play in the backyard, and they would repeat that to Maria. It wasn't long before I would hear them tell Maria those same excuses without asking me for permission first. They were starting to decide what they wanted to do and learning how to communicate that to Maria. And over time, the girls' relationship with Maria changed because they didn't really like Maria either, and they figured out how to be clear about how they wanted to spend their time.

✧ ✧ ✧

Just when it seemed like we had this friend thing figured out, things changed again. As the girls were in elementary school, they naturally made friends in their classrooms, and it wasn't long before they were invited to birthday parties. At first it was easy for me to just stay at the party and help out the hosting parent. Ashley was always happy to have me stay, just for reassurance. I started to notice fewer and fewer parents were staying at these parties, and many children just walked in all by themselves. I could see that in the future, I was going to have to give my daughters more freedom. But I was not was ready to have my child just walk into a stranger's house and stay with a mom who had not passed my inspection.

Then it happened.

Danielle was attending the eighth birthday party of her best friend, Madelyn. As we approached Madelyn's front door that morning, Danielle said, "Mom, you don't have to stay."

"I know, but . . ." I started to say as the door opened.

"Madelyn is so excited to have you Danielle," this mom said to Danielle. Then she turned to me, "Hi, I'm Joyce. You can come back at 11 to join us for birthday cake."

"I'm Lori," I managed to say before the door was closed without me moving. As I slowly turned to walk to the car, I thought, *how rude*. I realized I knew her daughter Madelyn very well from helping out at the school because the two girls were always together. I had seen Madelyn's mom at these events and we may have introduced ourselves a time or two, but we didn't even have our play date and she hadn't passed my inspection yet. I was not happy. I arrived home and complained to Dan about this. He calmly pointed out they seemed like a nice family. But I wasn't ready. Danielle was ready, but I wasn't ready.

I was back at Madelyn's front door right at 11. Someone opened the door; it was another mom who

Delegating Decisions

was picking up her daughter. She pointed out they were just finishing up presents. As I looked around, I saw Joyce, Madelyn's mom, wave and smile at me from across the room. Then I spotted Danielle in the mix of several little girls laughing and having a blast. The mom who I had passed as I walked in turned and said to me, "It is different just dropping our kids off at these birthday parties, isn't it? Brittany is our first and I am not quite used to this yet."

I agreed. "Danielle is our oldest, too. I guess we will get used to it, right?" I had a sick feeling in the pit of my stomach and the other mom nodded as she and her daughter walked out. As I continued to look around the room, I saw an older brother in the mix. Then it started to make sense. Joyce had already learned to let go a little more with her son. She was ready for this next step and I was not. I felt very comfortable in their house and I realized that Joyce would have passed my inspection. As the party ended, I watched Joyce remind Madelyn to say thank you as Madelyn and Danielle hugged and giggled.

"Did you have fun?" I asked as we got into the car.

Excitedly, Danielle told me every detail and didn't stop talking until we pulled into our garage. Then as she jumped out of the car she said, "Mom, thanks so much for letting me go all by myself."

Most of the time, your child is demanding freedom as you hold on tightly. Consider loosening your grip so you can be eased into the next phase.

I was frozen in my seat for a minute. I guess this was her decision, not mine, to make. I now realized I had to let go of my 'inspections'.

It seemed like it was the very next week that the phone started to ring. Madelyn wanted to know if Danielle was free to play together. In the blink of an eye, Ashley wanted to know why she couldn't call her friends to come play, too, and with that, we launched into a new phase. The phone would ring and someone's friend wanted to play. So with the friend holding on the other end of the phone, the girls would yell, "Hey Mom, can I play with my friend?"

It always seemed like I was making a snap decision, which sometimes worked out perfectly and other times would backfire entirely. Sometimes I wouldn't let the girls answer the phone when I saw who was calling on the caller ID because I wanted time to think. In the back of my mind, I remembered the situation with Maria when the girls would just do what she asked them to do, even if they didn't want to. They were still learning how to say no. With someone on the other end of the phone, how do I ask my girls what they wanted to do that day? How do I teach them to think for themselves? We needed time to think.

Then one day, each of the girls were calling a friend to come over to play. Ashley and Lindsey reported their success as they hung up the phone, but Danielle didn't say anything. Danielle called Brittany and when she hung up, she seemed sad. I asked, "Can't she come?"

"I don't know. She has to ask her mom and call me

back," she said. In a few minutes, the phone rang and Danielle answered it. She excitedly handed it to me and said, "Brittany's mom wants to talk to you."

We discussed details of the time and travel arrangements for the girls to play together that day. What's more, I was excited since an answer to my problem appeared before me. While the girls were all playing with friends that day, I started a list: who, what, start time, end time, and phone number. I made an index card with these prompts clearly written on it. I found a pad of paper, and put it and the card, along with a few pens, by the phone. At the end of the day after all the friends went home, I shared my index card with the girls.

We read it together, "Who? What? Start time? End time? Phone Number? I'll ask my mom and call you back."

They tried to guess what this card was for, but had no idea. I told them, "This card is going on the wall right by the phone. When your friends call you, you have to ask them these questions. Write down their answers. Then tell them you have to ask your mom and call them back. You MUST hang up before you come to ask me."

"That's stupid. I am NOT going to do that," was their first response.

"That is fine, then my answer to you is no," I explained with a little frustration. They looked confused, so I explained further. "No, you can't play with your friend today. Anytime you don't do this, then my answer will be no." I could both see their confusion and feel my frustration building, so I went and got the pad of paper I placed by the phone and began role-playing with each girl.

They started to have so much fun, that they continued to practice with each other while I went to start supper. While I cooked, they came running in and out of the kitchen to ask my pretend permission. I used this opportunity to teach a little more.

I asked Lindsey, "Do you want to play with Lindsey tonight?"

She pointed out that she was just pretending, but I said, "Just because someone asks you to play doesn't mean you want to play, even if I give you permission. If you want to play, you can call her back and tell her yes." I was lucky that when I saw her confusion, I had remembered to teach only one lesson at a time.

At supper that night, we shared the new rule with Dan. They demonstrated how it worked, and they were excited with their new skill of taking notes. After supper, we put the pad of paper, pens, and the card on the wall by the phone. We were ready.

At first, they carefully wrote all the answers to the questions on the notepad. Sometimes, they totally forgot and would ask me while their friend was still on the phone. I would just remind them to get the details and call back. An added benefit was the girls learned how to take messages when they answered the phone for me when I wasn't able to get to the phone. (Now that is a lost art. No more taking messages for others, since we all just leave voicemail.)

I was so relieved to have time to think. I could figure

out what our family plans were for the day, like if we were going to go to the park or had planned to spend the day at home-- all before my day was planned *for* me by my child and her friend. Sometimes we had options, so I would give that choice to the child. *Do you want to go to Brittany's house or to the park with your sisters?* I realized it didn't matter to me, so why not let Danielle decide.

I quickly realized a parallel that I'd seen in the girls' relationship with Maria. If they didn't feel like playing with that friend, they didn't know how to say no. They truly thought I would make them tell their friend that they wanted to play with them. I pointed out all they had to say, was, "Not today." They didn't need to give a reason or an excuse beyond that.

Sometimes *they* needed time to think. They were excited in the moment, but they were not sure what to do. In those instances, I told them we were going to wait five minutes and then we would talk about our decision. At the end of the five minutes, we talked through the options and it was easy for them to pick. We were not making snap decisions and I was giving them time to think, too.

> *Develop a method that gives you time to think, so you're not forced into a snap decision.*

It wasn't long before I started hearing them just tell their friend on the phone, "Not today."

They didn't ask the questions or come to me to

get permission. They just decided they didn't want to play. When I asked them what that was all about, they pointed out it was easier just to say what they wanted to do than to go through all of those steps. To them, they were choosing the easy route; to me, they had learned to make their own decisions.

Other times, there were the phone calls to me when they were at a friend's house, and were asking to play longer. I quickly learned to talk to a parent to see if they had approved of the extra time. I knew that with social Lindsey, she would often want to stay way past her welcome, so it was always good to check with the parents. Sometimes it was a scheme the girls thought would work. But if the parents had given permission, many times I was okay with it, since everyone was having a good time.

Then, one day, that backfired.

One Saturday, Danielle called and asked to stay longer at her friend Amanda's house. Amanda's parents were fine with the decision, so I let Danielle stay another few hours to play. Now, though, on Sunday, Danielle was mad at me that I let her stay at Amanda's house all day Saturday. She told me she felt like she had no time for herself all weekend. I explained that *she* had asked *me*, but she said it was just too long. As an introvert, Danielle needed time by herself to regroup and recharge, as she gets her energy from being alone. So the next time she called me to stay longer, I asked her on the phone if she was sure. She convinced me she was having fun, so I allowed her to stay longer.

Delegating Decisions

Later that day, she was out of sorts, ultimately and simply overwhelmed. Again she was mad at me for making her play at her friend's house all day! I was sure it was her idea to stay longer, I was confident she called me and begged to stay longer, but somehow it was still my fault.

We discussed what had happened and that I *had* asked her on the phone. She said she did at the time, because she was having fun. Then I remembered which child I was talking to: Danielle, the pleaser. If her friend wanted to play longer, then that was what she wanted . . . *at the time*. She was putting her friend's feelings before her own and couldn't think ahead to what her true needs were.

Together, Danielle and I decided that she would *never* be allowed to stay longer at a friend's home. The answer was always no. We made a plan ahead of time, and discussed exactly how much time she wanted to have with her friend. Then, if she called me explaining she was having a blast and wanted to stay longer, I would say no. When the time was up, she was done. That plan worked out so much better for her and her needs; I was just the enforcer. Of course, in time she started saying no to her friends without calling me first. She was not only learning to communicate to them directly, but she was also learning to put her needs above her friends. Her friends understood that Danielle was a planner and always stuck to the plan.

Being a social butterfly, Lindsey always enjoyed being with her friends, and it seemed she never tired of hanging out with them. She would get together with friends as often as I would let her. It wasn't long before all of the girls hosted and attended sleepovers. At first it was nice to have them hang out with friends all night instead of having to go out to pick them up. What I couldn't stand was the crabby kid(s) I was left managing the next day. I quickly decided that if they couldn't act normal around us, then they wouldn't be having any more sleepovers. The girls found that the best solution was to spend a great deal of time the next day in their rooms, away from their parents and sisters. Many times they would read and fall asleep, which is actually what they needed.

✧ ✧ ✧

As teenagers, friends became very important to the girls, but as it is in teenagerdom, sometimes those friendships had struggles. I told the girls that I would listen to their problems without judging and I could keep a secret. They never really believed me, until I realized I was not really telling the truth. So I changed my words to, "I will just listen, offer you some suggestions, that you can choose to use, or not. I will keep whatever you tell me a secret unless it is not safe to do that." They looked confused, so I continued, "If you tell me something that your friend might do that would be dangerous to themselves or others, then I will not keep the secret. But I will tell you before I do share that information."

After I was more honest with them, they seemed to trust me more. They shared their issues with getting along with their friends. When Ashley was in junior high, she struggled with knowing what was appropriate. She kept thinking she was hurting her friends' feelings because she could be a little too honest, so I would have her practice how to say things. For a few weeks, we had this conversation every day. Then she started feeling more comfortable, and then those questions came only once in the while. Even today, she still asks how to handle social situations; it just doesn't come naturally to her.

Danielle always wanted everyone to get along and because of that, I worried she would follow the crowd too much. In high school, though, she proved me wrong. While planning prom, one friend told a sub-group of friends that they were no longer invited to be a part of the 'prom group.' Danielle stepped in and told her friend that what she did "was hurtful and wrong." She added, "I will not be a part of the 'prom group' if the others are intentionally excluded."

Of course that caused friendship drama with people picking sides, but Danielle didn't care. She explained to me, "Mom that is just not a thing you do to friends. You don't tell them they are uninvited."

Danielle stood up for her convictions. She never wanted people to be hurt. It reminded me of the time when she was in third grade a couple of teenage boys were walking by our house, smoking. She said, a little too loudly, "Mom, those boys are smoking. Don't they know it will kill them? I think I should tell them. What if they don't know it will kill them?"

When Danielle was really upset or saw injustice, she did not hold back her emotions. In a way, that comforted me, but there was a part of me that worried she might get herself beat up. Thankfully that didn't happen!

Lindsey had a small group of great friends that she had since she was in second grade. She hung out with them as often us parents would allow. They all seemed to love doing the same things and the parents seemed to have the same values. I thought those relationships would last all through high school, but I was wrong. At the end of ninth grade, those friends turned on Lindsey. Girls can be so mean and they were. Lindsey felt like she had no friends, and her heart was broken. As her mom, I couldn't comfort her. I couldn't make it better. My heart broke for her. She survived the last few days of the school year, but then summer started, and Lindsey sat in the house, bored and sad. Clear as day, I remember her looking up at me from the couch as she had been staring out the living room window, and said, "This is going to be the longest summer of my life."

I had no magic wand that I could use to fix it. I had no answers for her.

> *Every now and then you can't fix it.*
> *All you can do is love them.*

How does a teenager find new friends in the summer? What could I do to help this social child? I didn't have much to offer, but Lindsey did play softball, so she practiced pitching. I even decided to talk to Danielle and Ashley. I told them that their sister was hurting, and I asked them to please be nice to her, and whenever possible, include her with some of their activities. They said they would be nice to her, but she couldn't hang out with their friends. I understood that I couldn't make them, but it didn't stop me from wishing I could!

That summer, the answer for Lindsey came in the form of a Mission Event at our church. She attended and was able to deepen her friendships with her church friends. In addition, she was able to talk to other teenagers about her mean friends. That week at church ended up being a big blessing in Lindsey's life.

Dictator Turned Advisor

It was always an unspoken expectation at our house that the girls would all go to college. Dan and I both attended college and we raised our girls with the assumption they would attend college, too. There was never an 'if'... it was always only a 'where?' question. In a flash, the time came for each of them to decide which college to attend. This was the first major decision that was determined by the girls alone. With Danielle, it was an emotional decision. She fell in love with the college, the major, the state, the town, everything. As we walked through the middle of the campus, I asked her, "Can you see yourself here?"

"Could I see myself?" She asked, a little confused.

I continued to explain. "Can you visualize walking across this campus next fall? Can you see yourself walking through the snow; see the mud in the spring? Do you feel like this could be your new home next fall?"

With all of the excitement of a blossoming 17-year-old, she said, "Oh, yes Mom for sure! It just feels right. When I visited last spring with the church youth director, it was a fun and neat place, but I wasn't excited then. Now, I am *so* excited. I think it is perfect."

I knew it was right for her, too. I saw it in her eyes and with the smile on her face. What she didn't know as I looked away was that I had made myself cry with my questions of next year, her independence, and her 'new' home. I was sad to be letting her grow up, but she was excited.

Danielle's excitement remained, even as she started looking for a second choice school. I kept reminding her that she had to wait and see if we/she could afford that private school she loved. She had to have a backup plan, just in case. One of the schools we visited was during a family trip, so Ashley was along. That university was not at all right for Danielle, but Ashley was very interested in that school. We had planted a seed for Ashley.

Meanwhile, Danielle was getting frustrated with the search; she was done looking. She picked a second school and I knew she didn't really like it. I had her talk to Dan about her choice. Both of them ended up frustrated. Dan said, "Fine, I won't give her any more advice if she doesn't want my opinion."

Danielle ended up in tears because her dad didn't listen. Over time, I was able to realize that it was her choice and not our choice. I pointed out to Dan that she didn't want advice; she just wanted him to listen. She wanted him to hear her reasoning and her thoughts. She didn't want him to fix it; she wanted his support. That he understood, but a Dad's role is to fix it. But I pointed out that perhaps not anymore. She had picked her second choice, whether we liked it or not.

> *When advising them, as they make their own decision, ask and listen. Don't tell.*

Full of nervous excitement, Danielle completed her applications to both schools. We completed all of the financial aid requirements and waited. Dan, the worrier, created a plan for our parent responsibility for college education for all three girls, which was made up of what we had set aside and what we could afford to borrow for each child. He knew we couldn't just start paying for the first one's dream to come true and have nothing left for the last one. And we both knew we would have a year with all three in college at the same time. Planning was a necessity.

Finally, the financial package arrived from her dream school . . . and Danielle burst into tears. The tuition was so high; could we/she really afford it? Dan was back on the computer, breaking down the cost per year, putting together an spreadsheet with the finances we would be putting into her education and the reminder that would be her responsibility. Meanwhile, I was trying to deal with Danielle's emotions and trying to console her until Dan could finish with the numbers. What Danielle was asking was so important: *"Could she afford it? How could she afford it?"*

It was exciting to hear that she understood it was her responsibility, though I was heartbroken that we/she may not be able to afford her dream school. I was also dealing with my own shock that this day was here. It was like those financial papers were her ticket away from me. I was also grieving the loss of my little girl. I was not helping the situation.

When Dan had finished with the numbers, he sat down and talked with Danielle. She reviewed everything and took the print-out to her room. She still had her heart broken that it wouldn't work. It was hard to stay away, but I, too, was emotionally exhausted. I wasn't sure what else I could say or do.

Soon Danielle came back out with her own breakdown. She had figured out how much it would cost her a month, but she didn't know what that number meant. She didn't know if that was a huge number or normal number in adult expenses. Dan explained to her that it would be like a car payment for 10 years. She still looked confused, so I clarified to her: "When you are done with college, other kids might be able to afford a new car, and you would need to have a cheap, used car. Other kids may be able to have a one-bedroom apartment on their own. You may need to share an apartment or have a studio apartment so you could pay your college loans."

"Oh, I could do that," she said with a smile.

"Is your dream school worth that?" I asked.

She looked at her dad. He reminded her it was entirely her decision, that only she could decide how much this school was worth to her future.

"I think so," she said.

"I think so, too," Dan replied.

That was all the encouragement she needed. All her sadness turned into excitement. Without another word, she smiled and hugged me. Through my tears of excitement and sadness, I hugged her back. Danielle's first big decision was made!

✧ ✧ ✧

In just the blink of an eye, we were repeating this whole process. I was shocked to find out that Ashley had already made her decision. When we visited that university as a family while Danielle toured schools, the seed that we planted had taken root and grown into a sturdy tree. That is where Ashley was going to go.

"But we need to check other possibilities and we need to visit that university again," I insisted.

"Why? I am NOT going to change my mind!" she demanded. She didn't understand that it was just about making sure. It wasn't about changing her mind, but she didn't get that. If I had asked Dan, I am sure he would have agreed with Ashley, but he knew not to question my persistence. If I thought we should be sure and check out other options, then that was what we were going to do, no matter if either of them wanted to or not. And we did. I also pointed out that we had to have a backup college just in case.

Ashley was hurt. "You think I am stupid and won't get in that university?"

Now I was really in trouble, and couldn't think of a logical excuse, so I just said, "Of course you will get in . . . you just always need a backup plan."

Visiting college campuses Ashley knew she wouldn't like was not a fun experience. Dan tried hard to support me on them, but his heart was not in it either. After just two campuses, we returned to visit to her university of choice. Ashley was still irritated that we had to waste time visiting again, but it was better than the other campuses. As we walked in the middle of the campus, I asked her, "Can you see yourself here?"

"Why wouldn't I?" she wondered. She couldn't relate to my question at all. It just wasn't how she was programmed. Dan tried to translate for me since he and Ashley thought alike. "She wants to understand what you like about it and what you don't."

"Like a pros and cons list?" she asked.

He agreed. Even though that was not at all what I was asking, I agreed, figuring that was as close as I would get with their logical brains. So that night, Ashley did what I asked, like a homework assignment. I thought at least I was helping her think through her decision. I am sure all she was thinking the whole time was, "This is so stupid. My decision is made so why is Mom making me do this? Doesn't she believe me?"

Ashley was rethinking her major, so her biggest reason to attend this university was because it gave her options if she did switch majors. It was a great university and it was close to extended family. I thought it was right for her. I didn't agree with her process, but that was beside the point; I had to learn to let her do it her way.

Ashley was excited to finally complete her university application. When I asked about sending in her application for her second choice, she didn't think she wanted to do that. She used logic to explain to Dan and me why she didn't need to apply to two schools. "I am going to get into the university. I really want to go to the university. We know exactly how much it is going to cost, and about how much we will get in financial aid because of Danielle's numbers, so we know I can afford it. So why do we want to throw away the application fee to the other college?"

Even though Dan agreed, he knew not to say anything. He just looked at me. I was tired of fighting them both and said, "Fine."

Ashley was right. She did get into the university, and the financial aid package was better than we expected because of Danielle also being in college. I didn't have the emotional reaction I did with her older sister. I figured that was because I had already adjusted to Danielle being out of the house, I was tired of the struggle, and I was just plain exhausted.

Ashley did switch majors by the time she registered for her first semester of classes. She had one friend that was also going to the university, but they both decided to live in different dorms to force themselves to get out and make new friends. Ashley started college excited and determined to make it work.

This all came crashing down on her as the semester wore on. Ashley is not one to express her emotions, so she just kept pushing on until Thanksgiving. We heard about a class she was struggling with and a TA who was not helpful. And at Thanksgiving break, she didn't want to ride back to campus a day early with her friend. Then she asked if I would please drive her back that Sunday afternoon.

There was something in her tone that told me she needed me. I agreed to the 500 mile round trip, and I could spend a night at mom's before heading back. Dan and I agreed she just needed more time at home, plus time in the car was always a great place to talk. We had a great trip back, and I asked as many questions as I could possibility think of. It seemed like all that was stressing her out was that one class . . . at least that's what I thought as we hugged goodbye and I dropped her off at her dorm.

That night, she called me while I was at my mom's. She was in tears.

"Mom, I am not happy here. I can't do it. I am failing my classes. I have no friends. Can I just go back home with you tomorrow and go to a community college next semester?"

"It can't be that bad," I said. My head was spinning between what was said in the car and what she was saying now on the phone. I reminded her of the good things she said in the car. We talked out her feelings and specifics. It was just one class; all the rest were fine. She didn't care she didn't have new friends and she was fine hanging out with her high school friend. Yes, her roommate was fine. After many questions and many tears on both sides of the phone, we found the real problem. She was homesick and failing one class. I knew she should just tough it out for the first year, but the words that came out of my mouth were, "You only have three weeks until the end of the semester."

"I don't think I can even make it that long," came her tearful response.

I was so happy I had said, 'just three weeks.' After a few more minutes of talking, she was feeling better. We decided to focus one day at a time. She asked, "Can I call you every day?"

"Of course," I said, shaking my head. Why didn't she know she could call me anytime? She was finally ready to focus on one day at a time and together we would make it to the end of the semester.

The next day, I made the return trip home, and as scheduled, we talked. She felt better than the night before, but was stressed with the class she was failing. We talked through some options for help. It was obvious she was struggling with asking for help. (Considering she had to call me on the phone to ask me for help after spending four days at home and a five-hour car ride, this was not a surprise!) I finally convinced her to go to her TA's office hours. She felt the TA was a jerk, so she didn't want to go, but she promised she would do it before we talked the next day.

That night, I was able to share with Dan this shocking situation. His first reaction, like mine, was that she should stick it out the full year. She had always struggled with transitions, and he believed that in time, she would adjust and thrive at the university. If not, she could apply to a different school the following year. I agreed logically with him, but he hadn't heard how desperate she was on the phone when she just wanted to come home. I told him I was worried. "What if next February she just quits? She is having trouble making it just three weeks."

I pointed out that this wasn't a logical decision, which are the kinds of things he understands better than I do. This was an emotional decision, which I understand better than he does. He agreed we would just focus on getting through this semester.

Ashley called every single day. At first, we focused on the class. She said she kept feeling like such a failure until I realized she was thinking that was how we felt. She thought we were disappointed in her. I was flabbergasted. I reminded her: "All Dad and I ever talk about is doing your best. It doesn't matter that this time your best was an F. It was still your best for this class, this professor, this TA, your freshmen year. It is okay, and we are still proud of you! Right now we just want you to make it through this semester!"

She finally heard me! She ultimately stopped beating herself up. She had done her best and would continue to do her best! She would work hard to make it through this semester one day at a time. Our daily conversations started looking into the future. Ashley wanted to move home in December, take a semester off to look for a different college, and just be home. I started asking her to focus on what was wrong with the university, what few things did she like, what size school would be better, etc. Ashley loved focusing on a future away from this university.

Little did Ashley know, Dan and I were not going to let her stay home the next semester. We truly believed that if Ashley quit and moved home, she would struggle with moving out again. She could commute to a local college, but we didn't believe that would have been right for her. Ashley thought about how happy she was at home and being with all of her high school friends, but that was not true. She hated high school, she had a love/hate relationship with her little sister, and most of her friends were not home anymore. Life had changed. But we knew she needed to feel that safety net.

I had to work hard at keeping my mouth shut and continue to support her choices, even if I was acting. The only way I was able to do that was to talk things out with Dan so I could share my true feelings. It also helped that I could roll my eyes because our communication was on the phone. And Ashley got through those three weeks with a call every single day.

When Ashley came home for the holiday, the plan was to see if she could find a new college during the break. She didn't think even if she found a new school, she could get registered and start by second semester. She didn't believe she could do all that in such a short time, but I was determined to get it done. I had already made a few calls to ask how she would go through the transfer process and what the deadlines were. (I didn't tell her that and made her find all that out on her own. This was her decision, but I had found out it was possible to do it within our time schedule.)

After being at home a week, Ashley came running down the steps, full of excitement. She announced, "I passed. I got a D in the class I was failing!" Both Dan and I congratulated her as she said, with tears in her eyes, "I never thought you guys would ever be happy with a D."

"After you graduate, no one is going to say, 'you got a D in that class?' They are going to just look at your overall grade point average. In the end, it won't matter," Dan pointed out.

That was the start of Ashley getting her confidence back. Right after New Year's, Ashley and I visited three colleges using the guidelines she had figured out through our phone calls. On our way home from the last one, Ashley said to me, "Mom, I can just see myself at the first one. It just feels right."

I was glad I was driving so I could look away because tears rolled down my cheeks. It really was about feelings, even with my logical child. Later I found out she didn't think I liked that college because I didn't say anything. She didn't know I didn't say anything because I was too happy and proud of her that I was too choked up to speak.

The next week, Ashley and Dan visited her new college to convince him this was the right thing to do. Dan wasn't sure if it was the right college and if it was the right time to change schools, right in the middle of her freshmen year. She was going from a large university

Delegating Decisions

to a very small college and we were worried she was just settling. It didn't take long for Dan to be convinced, because while they were there, Ashley completed her application process and signed up for classes for the next semester. By the beginning of the next week, we had moved Ashley out of the dorms at her university and into her new college. She was not only starting over, but was doing it with the confidence she gained from this whole experience.

> *Mistakes are a part of life, and they're hard lessons to watch your child learn. Remember, a mistake can become the thing that transforms them.*

✧ ✧ ✧

And, in just the blink of another eye, Lindsey was asking when she was going to have a turn to visit schools. We had only done one actual college visit in the fall, and Lindsey wanted to know, "If we could visit one this month." I had to admit I had forgotten it was really *her time* to get this done, so I was glad she was on top of it. She wanted to visit a state school that reminded me of the university that Ashley had just left. I was not excited about that, but I agreed to take a look. This state school was in the degree area Lindsey was focused on pursuing. I was off on my fourth college visit and my sixth drive to a campus that month. I spent most of the drive trying hard to erase all of the previous visits I had just been through with Ashley. I started to relax and enjoy the trip, as I realized that once Lindsey had made her selection, we would be done. This was my last child to send off to college.

Lindsey loved the campus, and she enjoyed the size of state school; she was so excited. I spent the entire day making a mental list of all the things the state school offered incoming freshmen to help them be more successful, things that the school Ashley had just left did not offer. I asked Lindsey so many questions about the size of the school and the possibility of getting lost in the crowd that she finally looked at me and said, "Mom, I am not Ashley. I am social. I will talk to everyone. I will get involved in all kinds of things."

"You are so right . . . thanks for the reminder," I said to her with a smile. I needed to be reminded. I was with my social butterfly, my not-afraid-of-anything-child. Lindsey would thrive with so many opportunities at her fingertips.

As we walked back across campus one last time, Lindsey looked around and said, "I know it may be too soon for me to say this, but I can see myself here next year. It just fits me."

"That's exciting," was all I could say. I looked away, and tears filled my eyes once again. Lindsey was my last baby, about ready to leave home, and she got it. She got the idea that you should just feel it. You will know when it is right.

Lindsey had played softball in high school and had dreams of playing softball in college. On the way home, I tried to point out that getting on a division one softball team may be hard to do. She might have to decide how important playing softball in college was to her. If that was something she really wanted to do, then perhaps she may want to visit one of the division three colleges.

"Mom, don't you think I am good enough?" she asked. She was hurt.

No matter what I said, I just kept making things worse. I unintentionally kept digging myself deeper in the hole. I was not trying to hurt her feelings, but I wanted her to be prepared for some possible disappointment. I tried to point out this dream may need to be part of her decision. Finally, we just dropped the conversation.

> *Sometimes when you are being realistic, it sounds like you don't believe their dream is possible.*

Lindsey visited a couple more colleges, and found another college she really liked. This one was smaller than the first one, but was still a large, out of state college. She completed her application process to both schools before her senior year even started. She didn't really have a first and second choice anymore; she liked them both equally. She was accepted to both, and spent the next several months trying to figure out which one to attend. It wasn't until she took a trip to one of the campuses in January with Dan that she made up her mind. As she was walking around the campus on a cold, windy day in January, that campus seemed like home. Dan knew the financial package would be similar between the two schools, so they talked about how it would work financially. She announced she was going to attend the state school and try out for the softball team in the fall as a walk-on. She believed she would be able to play freshmen softball and see where it went from there. "The idea is to get the right education," she reminded me.

As it turned out, she learned about a lot of activities she could get involved in on campus after she arrived. One of the activities she found was Club Ball. After talking to the person involved in Club Ball who used to be on the softball team, Lindsey decided Club Ball was more in line with what she wanted to do. She didn't want softball to control her college life. I hate it when my girls are smarter than I am!

> *Be prepared for your child to prove you wrong!*

Lindsey was right. She did fit right in and ended up loving Club Ball, as it fit better into her many other college activities.

In the Rearview Mirror of Delegating Decisions

Looking back, I am in awe that even as toddlers, the girls needed to start to make their own decisions. When I was so busy with my daily routine, I had no idea they were striving to make their own choices. I am sure the reason it is called the terrible twos is because we adults are trying desperately to control their choices. I know I was. I learned that controlling everything was not the answer. Limited choices, however, was the perfect place to start. I realize I sound like a control freak with their clothes and their outfits, and perhaps I was, but I think it was just the first thing the girls pushed to do themselves. And I kept resisting.

Friends became such an influential part of our girls' lives and I was compelled to guide their selections. As they got older, my guiding hand was pushed aside. I was lucky I was able to watch their interactions by having their friends into our home. Arranging friend time changed with text messaging. I still felt it was essential for the girls to come to me to discuss their plans, and not text me from school or outside to ask, 'Can I . . . ?' I found discussing the options face-to-face was crucial. As they became teenagers, my opinions were better off kept to myself because if they weren't, the girls would do the opposite of what I recommended.

I mentioned the girls didn't want to spend their own money on clothes. They had started to receive an allowance when they were in elementary school. They had to put a certain amount in each envelope to budget their money: school supplies, church donations, savings, and fun money (their money). They could use their fun money for whatever they wanted. As pre-teens, they didn't want to use their fun money for the special outfit I wouldn't buy. That's when I realized they understood the value of money.

Dan and I spent a great deal of time talking around the girls. They heard us make decisions about our day-to-day lives and talk out the pros and cons of major purchases. Of course, those discussions focused a great deal on finances. Sometimes they were even involved in the discussions as we determined what to do on a vacation. I didn't know it at the time, but that was preparing them to make their first major decisions on their own: where to go to college.

Chapter 11:
Letting Go

When Danielle was in college, she shared with me her insight about other parents. Her 20-year-old friends were struggling with over-protective parents. The young adults thought it was emotional abuse. These parents were unable to let go of their adult children, sometimes holding on too tightly. I started to wonder, *Why am I not that way?*

According to Danielle, it's because I waited to have children until later in life. (Little did she understand that I didn't wait by choice. I didn't have a man to be the father. I thought *I* was ready.) She understood I had an adult life without children and was looking forward to having it again. Some of her friends' parents had never been independent adults – they were dependent children living with or being controlled by their parents when they became parents. They didn't know any other role than that of being parents. The good news was, they were great parents who did teach their children to be independent. Now they just needed to let go, which was the greatest gift of all, and the most rewarding!

Now What?

Danielle crossed the stage as a college graduate with

a double major in English and Psychology. She had grown into an amazing young woman who freely shared her views on any topic. She was not afraid to stand her ground when others disagreed with her. She loved to debate, and was easily frustrated when others wouldn't listen to opposing ideas. She admired some of her professors, and vice versa. She loved her college, the friends she made there, and the town that she had called home for four years. She was leaving a place she loved and thrived at. But now it was time to move on.

As the ceremony continued, I started to feel the most powerful emotions. I was so proud of who she had become, all that she accomplished, and all of the dreams she had for her future. I was so swollen with pride that the tears just poured down my checks. Lindsey and Ashley looked up at me and just shook their heads with that, 'oh Mom' look. Dan glanced over and gave me a nod that he understood my tears, but he was on the other side of the girls and couldn't console me with a hug. I was relieved, because I think I would have bawled if he had. This intense feeling was hard to understand at first, until I realized that it also was a release years of fear. A mother's fear that college would mean the loss of a child through the choices they made. The fear that a phone call would come that no parent wants to think about, but secretly fears. As I looked at the graduation ceremony through my tears, I realized we had made it this far and the tears were also my release.

After the ceremony, I watched as Dan gave Danielle a hug and shared his proud dad look. The tears started again . . . but this time it was from a memory of my own father's hug when I had gotten my college degree. My dad only hugged me a handful of times, with my college graduation being one of them. He had given me that same proud dad look. Before I completely fell apart, I lifted my camera and started taking pictures. Hiding my face behind the camera gave me something else to focus on to control all of these emotions.

We enjoyed this special moment: nice weather, a celebration dinner, and being together as a family to share this day with Danielle.

This exceptional day drew to a close. After one car was loaded, Dan headed out with Ashley and Lindsey. Danielle finished cleaning up her room and saying goodbye to her friends, and I tried to stay out of her way and not rush her. This was her time to deal with her emotions.

Danielle filled with joy!

Soon we were on our way. As we drove, we shared our memories: about the first time we visited this college, her moving in, the hard first goodbye, and the adjustment to college. She shared her feelings about college life, the struggles she had, the lessons she learned, and the passion she had for her alma mater. I tried to listen more than talk, which is hard for me. I bit my tongue as it got quiet, as I realized she was saying her own goodbye to a chapter of her life.

What we didn't discuss was what was ahead of us. She was heading back to her parents' house, moving back into her old bedroom. In anticipation of her arrival, Dan had put up extra shelves in the storage room, and the family room was ready for her belongings.

The family room is the first room in our house off the garage. It had become the place to gather belongings before leaving or after returning from trips. This year, the family room saw a great deal of activity with all of the transition. Lindsey had arrived home with her freshmen year belongings the first week of May. She had one week to do laundry, sort, and put her things in her room or on a shelf in the storage room. Then Ashley arrived home from college with her junior year belongings. She, too, had one week to sort and arrange her belongings. When Danielle and I arrived home, the family room was half full of her possessions from the first car. We added our load to the pile. She was moved back in; not settled, but in.

At first, having all the girls home was exciting, sort of like a vacation. However, it didn't take long for me to notice the tension beginning to build. The girls had shared a car in high school; they called it Earl. (The car was their grandparents' used car, so it needed an old person's name.) Danielle had Earl at college for her senior year. Now she felt like Earl was her car, but her sisters felt like they still shared Earl. Luckily before the tension grew, Lindsey left to work in Florida for eight weeks that summer. Ashley started an internship at the company Dan worked at, so we thought they would go to work together. However, Ashley wasn't sure she wanted to do that every day, and Danielle assumed she would have 'her' car just sitting there, waiting for her. Of course, I assumed it was my job to jump in to be the referee, being put into the role with each of the girls coming to complain to me. (I am not sure if I was pushed or if I fell back into the Mom role.)

I needed to figure out arrangements that took me out of the conversations, so I made a weekly schedule on the blackboard wall in the laundry room. There was a column for Earl and my van. I wrote on the days and times I would use my van and the rest of the time they could drive it. They were to add their own schedules to the list for either Earl or my van.

At first, the schedule seemed to work, and most days, Ashley did car pool with her dad. But it didn't take long for the complaints to start again. This time, it was about who was getting Earl and who had to drive the van. I didn't get the logic of these complaints. I know a minivan looks like a mom car, but Earl was not a flashy car, either. Earl looked like an old person's car. What difference did it make? It wasn't until the summer was more than half over that a random conversation touched on the root of the problem.

One night at supper, Dan happened to mention someone at work was selling a car and he asked if we would need one for the fall. I said we might and we discussed the price. The girls wondered why we would need a car. We explained that Ashley would be taking Earl for her senior year of college, like Danielle did. Then, depending on where Danielle got a job, *she* may need a car. It was just a matter of facts for us, but to Ashley it was affirmation that she would get Earl, as promised. The disagreements over the car stopped. The real issue was the future of Earl, not the day-to-day summer schedule!

Danielle started the summer adjusting to this new chapter in her life. She attacked it in her own style, with reading, thinking, and lots of writing. She was and always would be a creative writer, but her real dilemma was *what to do now?* She was trying to decide how to juggle the need for full time employment with her dream she was pursuing. She had been accepted into the Peace Corps, but had more hurdles to jump through before she would be given an assignment. She needed to find a way to earn money, but she couldn't make a long-term commitment. Dan thought she should be applying to every job in her field until she got one. I was using my connections to share employment opportunities with her. We talked about the statistics where 25% of college graduates were not getting jobs and 50% were not getting jobs in their field because of the economy. Dan and I thought we were being very patient, but I am sure Danielle thought we just didn't get it.

> *Your adult children don't want to hear your expertise or job suggestions. Bite your tongue.*

Her days were filled with this personal search for direction and completing the hurdles of the Peace Corps process. She figured out that she wanted to spend her spare time using her creative side to write and get an active, more social job for income. If possible, it would be one that didn't use her creative brain, so she would have that left at the end of the day to do her writing. I was very impressed with the insight she discovered with her process, but what did this mean for employment now? I tried to bite my tongue, but I am sure she could sense my question. Dan and I talked behind her back about the people we knew who had graduated from college and were living at home with their parents; some had part time jobs, some went back to school. We worried about where Danielle was really headed.

By August, she found a retail job close to our house, a job that gave her the income she needed but one that she could leave when her Peace Corps dream became a reality. Danielle was relieved to have a job. She had been working since just before her 16th birthday. She always used her money to buy what she needed and didn't ask us for more. It wasn't until months later that I realized she had made it through those summer months without asking for spending money. Yes, we had paid for her groceries, if we went out to eat together we would buy, and we put gas in the car. But she never asked for money for a movie, to buy clothes, or visit friends. She made do with what she had in her account. She was a responsible adult. Our constant pressure for her to get a job wasn't about her. It was our own fear that we had not taught our child responsibility. What we didn't realize was she was showing us each day that she was already a responsible adult. We just didn't see it.

I wish I could say that the adjustment was over once Danielle got her job and found her work routine, but it was more complicated than that. She was back in a town she had grown to despise since she had left four years earlier. She complained about where she was living, often with a disclaimer, "I don't mind living with you, but in this town."

I had a hard time dealing with her unhappiness. As her mom, I tried to make it better, but I couldn't change what town we were living in. Then her unhappiness started to change into judgments about the way we did things around the house. I started to hear her question what foods we ate, what TV shows we watched, my messy office taking up the entire basement, doing nothing exciting on weekends, and when did we start eating supper in front of the TV? I knew she was just dealing with the emotions of having her new life and not having the exciting college campus at her disposal, but some days those questions hurt. Everyday life was sometimes boring and we may have developed bad habits, but I didn't ask for them to be pointed out to us in that way.

I could feel the tension within me building. There were days when she would come through the kitchen to get what she wanted and head straight back to her room. I would have tears in my eyes, wishing we could just have a cup of coffee in the same room. I felt like I was in her way. Other times, I would hurry to my basement office when I would hear her get up, just to stay out of her path because I didn't want to feel her judgment.

One morning, a similar scene played out. I stood in the kitchen, feeling like a pressure cooker ready to blow. This had to change, or I knew that one morning I would just yell at her for walking into the kitchen to get breakfast. How fair would that be?

I just didn't want her here.

Oh my God, did that thought just cross my mind? I didn't want my wonderful daughter living in our house? I felt tears fall rapidly down my cheeks. I was so disappointed in myself for having such a thought. Was this truly how I felt? I started to sob. I didn't want to feel this way. I wanted to enjoy having her here. This could be the last time we lived in the same house. This probably *was* the last time we would live in the same house. The sobbing stopped, but as the tears trickled, I realized it wasn't what Danielle was doing that was stressful. It was that the relationship I wanted wasn't there.

To develop it, I had to focus on my own attitude. I had to look at this opportunity to live together again as a gift and not an inconvenience. It was up to me to enjoy having her here. It was up to me to learn how to live with my adult daughter. Then she might learn how to live as an adult in her parents' home.

Communication would be the key, in addition to my own attitude adjustment.

> *Communication is the key to developing an adult relationship with your child.*

With my new awareness, I asked her if we could go to breakfast on her next day off. The two of us spent three hours at breakfast. We discussed her feelings about the suburb we lived in and how it was hard for me to hear about how much she disliked it. It was my town and I was still living here. I didn't want to focus on what was wrong with it. I didn't expect her to like it, but I had a hard time hearing about her distaste all the time. She pointed out that she liked the city, just not the suburb, and she realized she needed to go to the city more often.

We talked about what life was like the last time she was living at home. We had three teenagers, all in high school. Our evening meal was planned and eaten around the kitchen counter every day, or at the dining room table. There was one exception to that which was, 'make your own' night. That was when everyone got to eat what they wanted, when they wanted, and where they wanted. That was the only time we ate in front of the TV. She quickly asked, "What happened to that?"

"You left," I replied. "You don't understand that after you left, eating at the table or counter left an empty spot. Each night, we were reminded you were missing. Of course, we still did that most of the time, but the next year Ashley left, too. Then whenever we were eating at the counter, there were two empty spots. We still ate together at times, but it slowly just got easier to eat in the living room and not miss you guys. And the three of us never ate in the dining room; it was too lonely." I went on to point out, "This year it was just Dad and me, so we needed the TV to help us deal with this new emptiness."

As I shared this with her, I realized that was what had happened. It wasn't just a few bad habits that we had started. It was something we did subconsciously to cope. Danielle and I continued to discuss why she thought it was stupid to eat in front of the TV. I said that I agreed; besides, I was the one who taught her that. I agreed that we would work harder at eating more meals at the counter and with the TV off. She liked that idea.

I reminded her of the conversations we had when she was growing up. We would talk about what was bothering her and how we were just not getting along. Sometimes the issue was me nagging her to go to bed, and she would remind me she could read a clock and get ready for bed on her own without me saying it was bedtime.

"I would tell you, 'you are my oldest, so sometimes you have to teach me how to be a mom of this age child.' I promised you I would learn, but sometimes you had to push me to get it." We shared a few of those stories and I felt our connection growing.

"I am learning how to be a mom of an independent adult. I am struggling to remember not to give advice. I need your help to point out what I am doing wrong," I shared.

"You need to stop giving advice and trying to fix everything," she quickly answered. She had been feeling the tension, too.

"Yes, I do that," I replied. "I feel it is my job as a mom, but it is also what I do with my friends. With my friends,

I learned to wait for them to ask for my opinion and not just give it. As a mom of an independent adult child, I will have to learn to wait for you to ask me. I will try very hard, but you may need to remind me at times."

We ended our breakfast with the beginning of a new relationship. I knew I would need to work at it, but I could already feel the rewards for the effort.

I am not sure how many times I had to be given the look as I started to give her advice, and I would try hard to stop mid-sentence. I am not sure how many times I failed to even notice, but I know that over time, things got better. I knew we were heading in the right direction when one morning Danielle came into the basement to ask me what the plans were for supper. I felt instant frustration hit, as I replied with an attitude, "I don't know."

She rolled her eyes and turned to walk out. I quickly called after her and said, "Wait, let's talk about this quickly." I shared my insight, "This was a mom-teenage daughter conversation and that is not what we want. Can you ask me again and I will listen to my adult daughter?"

She nodded and said, "I just want to know what is for supper so I can decide what to take for lunch, or if I should get something on my way home if I don't want to eat what you are having."

I explained, "That makes sense. But I get frustrated because I am in the middle of my work morning and have not yet thought about supper. I feel like you are pointing out my mom-failure. But I now realize you just want information, and it must be frustrating not knowing. I am sure you hesitate in asking me because

I give you attitude when you ask and I don't have an answer. For tonight, let's do make your own. Later today, I will work on a menu plan for the week so everyone will know what to expect."

She was happy for that solution as she headed back upstairs to get ready for work. I was not only relieved that we had found a way to get the *'what's for supper'* monkey off my back, but we also discussed a frustration as two adults. Communication was the key. Soon, I had a fancy menu board with meals planned for the week ahead and I tried new recipes and even focused on a vegetarian dish once a week. Danielle was thrilled with my efforts and stopped complaining on the nights we had things she didn't like because she knew what to expect.

Our morning routine went from being a dance of avoidance to a special time we shared together. We both enjoyed our coffee and breakfast in the living room. Sometimes we were on our own and sometimes we were together. Then one day, I closed my laptop and told her I better head downstairs to get to work and give her some space.

She said, "No, stay with me."

I asked if she was sure. She explained it was nice to have me working in the room with her. She went to grab her writing so she could work, too. As she left the room, a tear slid down my cheek. We had made it. We were two adults sharing space and respect. We even developed a coffee rule: if you were up, you asked the other one if they needed a refill before you sat back down. It always feels good to get a refill without having to get up.

It wasn't long before I was treasuring those mornings. Danielle was going to be leaving for the Peace Corps soon and she would be gone for 28 months. As that day was getting closer, I said to her that I was mad at her for spoiling my coffee drinking time. I said that every day from now on I would think of her when I had to fill my own coffee in the morning. She told me I could quit, and I said, "Never."

A month after she left for South Africa, in her first report back to her family and friends, she shared that she didn't drink coffee anymore. Her last cup of coffee was the one I had put in a travel mug for her to have on the way to the airport. She handed me back the empty travel mug as we said our last farewells. Could it be that her drinking coffee made her miss me too much, just like us eating at the counter with an empty stool?

> *Treasure the everyday moments; they will be gone before you know it.*

Bite my Tongue

In just the blink of an eye, I was sitting at Ashley's last Symphonic Winds Concert. In less than two weeks, she would be receiving her Bachelor of Arts in Computer Science degree. As we waited for the concert to start, Dan and I discussed all the concerts we had attended. How hard it was to be proud parents of fifth and six graders at their first concerts. The students sounded like they were each playing their own songs. But we proudly smiled as we listened, clapped more than politely, and talked on the way home about which song was the best one. Each year, the concerts sounded better and we were truly proud parents as we listened. We talked about how breathtaking Ashley's Symphonic Winds concerts had been. We were looking forward to hearing this last concert.

We reminisced about how little Ashley looked holding her first alto saxophone. It was so big for her, but she loved to play it. Like most kids, she didn't like to practice, but she had a natural talent for it. However, she was quickly bored with the alto saxophone and moved to the tenor saxophone. Then when the college band needed a baritone saxophone, she jumped at the chance to play yet another style of saxophone. Now that little girl was all grown up and playing the baritone saxophone at her last concert.

Ashley's last concert

As they walked onto the stage, those years flashed before me as tears filled my eyes. I was sad for Ashley, knowing how much she enjoyed playing her saxophone and realizing it would be hard for her to keep that hobby in the future. My feelings were quickly transformed to joy and happiness as they began to play. The performance was incredible! This time we were overwhelmed with pride as we listened to her last concert. I was able to keep my emotions under control until they had each of the seniors stand for recognition. I quickly hid my eyes behind my camera as I snapped a picture. Dan and Danielle gave me a sweet smile as they saw me wipe my tears.

Ashley's graduation felt more like a stepping-stone than the end of a chapter. She was ready to be done with college life. She had spent the last six months applying to jobs, attending interviews, and determining the right job for her. She had asked for guidance and advice from both Dan and me. She appreciated our suggestions and recommendations, but knew the final decision on which job to accept was hers to make. She had set a goal before the start of her senior year to have a job by spring break. She didn't quite make that goal, but a month after spring break she accepted the job she wanted. Ashley would be starting her professional career at a company just 20 miles from our house, three weeks after graduation.

Ashley had a plan to get an apartment with her boyfriend as soon as he found his job. She figured she would be moving into her own apartment before she started work, or at the latest, within that first month. When I explained to her that she could stay at home until she got her feet on the ground, she said sarcastically, "Mom, that is why I went to college . . . so I could move home and stay with my parents."

> *Remember you want your child to be independent, even if they are pushing you away.*

I knew as I watched her cross the stage to receive her Bachelor of Arts in Computer Science degree that she was a very independent adult, ready for the world ahead. But my mind started to wander to her freshman year when she wanted to quit. She survived, she adjusted during a college transfer, and she thrived at her new college. She had struggled to ask a TA for help, and then she became a TA and helped underclassmen. She became a leader in the computer science department. She wasn't the same girl we had dropped off at this new college three and half years earlier. She was now a self-determined, ambitious young lady.

Our family had a wonderful weekend celebration for Ashley's college graduation. Ashley and her boyfriend hosted a family picnic for both families to kick-off the weekend. We ended the festive weekend with dinner at Ashley's favorite restaurant with the five of us, and we had a very special time. As I cherished this extraordinary time together, I decided I wanted one more weekend. I asked, with tears in my eyes, "Can we have one last family camping trip together next weekend? I just want one more weekend together as a family."

They could all tell that I was more than asking; I was demanding one more Forced Family Fun weekend. When I mentioned to Ashley that she could invite her boyfriend, she was excited to commit. That surprised everyone since she hated camping, but her boyfriend liked it. Everyone else soon joined in the excitement. They could tell this was important to me. It was the last weekend Lindsey would be home before she headed to work at summer camp. Danielle was leaving in six short weeks for the Peace Corps, and Ashley would be starting full time employment in just two weeks. A new chapter was about to begin.

Our camping weekend was my weekend to adjust. I spent most of the time thinking back to when they were little. Our first camping trip had been 15 years earlier, when we had to worry about them falling into the bonfire or teaching them how to fish. We all shared past adventures. I listened to their deep conversations and advice to each other, and knew I was seeing a glimpse of their future relationships. I witnessed how adding boyfriends into the mix was an addition to the family. We had fun and silliness as we continued to laugh at each person's unique chuckle, giggle, or snort. I was able to witness the girls' admiration for each other, something I never thought would happen when they were little and fighting over everything. Their relationship as siblings had grown to adulthood, too.

> *A cherished moment is watching siblings get along.*

◆ ◆ ◆

Just after our weekend, Ashley asked Dan and I about our plans for Earl. Danielle had had Earl for her senior year of college. Ashley had possession of it the last nine months of her senior year. Lindsey was only going to be a junior the next year, so she shouldn't be expecting Earl for another year. Who would be using the car now? Lindsey would be at camp all summer, and Danielle would be gone in just a month. We quickly determined that Ashley needed Earl to get to work. It made sense to let Ashley keep Earl until she was ready to buy her own car. She was very excited about that. She was hoping she could wait until she had a little money saved up so she could buy a new car instead of having to purchase a used car right away. Dan and I told her to plan to use Earl as long as she needed to. (As it turned out, Ashley got a new car in December and Lindsey got to use Earl after spring break in her junior year.)

I adjusted to having the adult Ashley home much easier than when Danielle moved home. I am sure my experience with Danielle helped enormously. Plus, Ashley wasn't going to be with us long. She had a plan to move out as soon as her boyfriend got a job. I discussed with Ashley my new menu plan, where I would write down what we would have for dinner each day and she could plan accordingly. She asked if she could cook her own meals. She liked to cook and most of the time didn't like what I made. As I bit my tongue and tried to hide my hurt feelings, I agreed that that would be fine.

As Ashley started her new job, she adjusted to a longer commute than anticipated due to road construction. I offered her some alternative routes and she settled on the best one. I am not sure if I was asked my opinion, but I gave it. I was quickly reminded of how scheduled she was.

I never had to guess what she would be doing. I could stay out of her way and she loved it when I did. I am not that scheduled, but I could work around her schedule, such as never do laundry on Saturday afternoon, since that's when she did her laundry. She had made her bedroom her space. She had her own TV and even ate most of her meals in her room. It was hard to have her home but totally in her own space. I missed her more having her just upstairs. When I could no longer take it, I would make her favorite food and ask if she could like to join us. It usually worked so we could all eat together.

On one such night, I was finishing up our dinner and Ashley was upstairs. I got a text from her that said, "Sorry, I won't be eating supper with you. I just broke up with my boyfriend and want to be left alone. I am not going to get an apartment with him and I will be living at home forever."

I had to remind myself that Ashley was an adult and had the right to deal with this her own way. But as her mom I wanted to go to her and give her a big hug. She was just upstairs. I had to bite my tongue and give her space to deal with it. I offered in a text that Dad and I could go for a walk and she could come get some food. She replied, "No, I am not hungry and I just want to stay in my room, **alone**."

As a mom, leaving things alone is the hardest thing for me to do. I just have to fix it. But she had told me to leave her alone. Each day that I succeeded at staying out of her way and not saying anything, I was proud of myself. Finally, after three days, which to me felt like a lifetime, I knew I had to say something. If I didn't, I would start offering tons of mom advice, which I kept thinking about. I could only bite my tongue for so long.

I went to her and asked if I could talk to her about what had happened. We had a nice adult-to-adult conversation. I was so happy she was willing to share with me and talk about what her future options were now. I had to wipe a few tears from my eyes as my mom pride started to seep out. She was all grown-up and ready to be out of her parents' house. We started to talk about where she wanted to live and if she wanted to live on her own or with friends. I offered my mom advice; I thought she would love to get an apartment by herself. She loved having her space and her own schedule without others getting in her way. This might be the only time in her life she would really be on her own. I had loved living on my own before I had gotten married, and perhaps she would, too.

I could tell from the look in her eyes that it was time for me to bite my tongue again. So I did. We sat quietly for a while and then I left, thanking her for sharing with me. Later that night, she asked me if I would come with her to look for apartments. I was thrilled. I was growing into my new mom role!

No Longer Teenagers
The girls were no longer teenagers. As we celebrated Lindsey's 20th birthday, Danielle congratulated her by saying, "Congratulations, you made it. You are not a teenage mother."

"Yep, we all made it," Lindsey replied with a laugh. She continued as she looked at Dan and me, "Congratulations, you raised your girls through their teenage years without a pregnancy."

"I didn't know it was something we had to worry about," was my quick response. Then I added my parental advice, "I am not sure it is a success unless we make it to no premarital pregnancy. And I don't want to see that comment on Facebook!"

Lindsey at 20 already!

That conversation echoed in my mind as we drove back home that evening. As parents, we had raised our three girls into their twenties. We did it. We didn't have a teenage pregnancy. We didn't have to deal with total disobedience, sneaking out of the house, smoking, drug use, and alcohol consumption in high school. We had succeeded. Was it really us? Did we have the tools, talent, and skill, or was it luck? Then I felt a Presence over me, reminding me it wasn't luck. It was God. We had our faith and prayers every step of the way to guide our girls, our responses to them, and their actions.

As the quiet drive continued, I realized I was confused. We, as their parents, didn't really know what they did each day. What happened that we didn't know about yet? Many of their teenage stories were yet to be shared with us, if ever. We didn't know the many actions that they did when we, their parents, were not around. We didn't know about the fears they kept to themselves or the inner struggles they kept deep in their hearts. As that realization started to overtake me, I remembered that our job as their parents was not to keep all pain and difficulties from them. Our job wasn't to protect them from pain and sadness. Our job was to give them the skills to cope. Our job was to be their support, either by physically holding them through their sadness, or by them emotionally knowing we were there and always would be there for them, no matter what. Then, a proud tear slid down my check. I finally understood that even the things we didn't know about, the secrets that were still kept from us were also a sign that we had succeeded. Our girls had grown up.

> *A parent's job is NOT to protect their children from every difficulty, but to provide them with the skills to cope.*

In the Rearview Mirror of Letting Go

Looking back, as I left a job I would evaluate it: what kind of job did I do? How did I improve the lives of others? Was I leaving behind something more than they had before I arrived? The most important question was, were they able to carry on without me? As my job as a Full-time Mom role ended, I realized that I would have left an impact on the girls, no matter what type of job I did. Did I scar them for life or did I enhance their character? I believe my willingness to keep trying and learning along the way helped me support their development into their unique personalities. Did I give them the skills to be on their own? As they each moved back home for a short time, the adjustments were NOT smooth. This was proof they were used to being independent, young adults and not hearing mom advice or guidance every day.

The true question is what type of job did I do? I made mistakes, asked for forgiveness, and never gave up, which taught them to be confident, successful women. They have demonstrated that by going after their dreams, hitting setbacks, coping and moving forward again. I watch them continue to go after their dreams and let no one stand in their way, not even me.

I can no longer say I am a Full-time Mom since the girls are all over 21. Danielle, 24, is still serving in the Peace Corps in South Africa.

My adult girls: Lindsey, Ashley, and Danielle

Her email updates are professional stories with insight and inspiration of a world I don't understand. She is contemplating extending her stay for an additional year. Ashley, 23, is a Software Engineer and has her *own apartment just 20 minutes away from us. We enjoy sharing Sunday dinners together and singing in the same adult choir at church. Ashley has developed into an amazing professional woman. Lindsey is 21 and a senior in college. She has already demonstrated her independence by spending five weeks on a summer mission trip to Namibia, Africa. As she packed to be the team medic contact, she felt like a mom, thinking of what the others might need. In a few short months, Lindsey will be receiving her Bachelor of Science Degree in Religious Studies. She already has plans to participate in a two-year internship at a camp in Colorado.*

It is obvious they can easily carry on without me; they are on their own. I am proud to call each of them my daughters. I am, however, still their mom. I continue to listen without giving advice, or I at least wait for them to ask . . . most of the time. I will always be here for them. Many times a text comes in that brings me back to my role, 'Mommy Fix It!' I am honored to share my Mom Advice. And I always treasure their reply texts: "Thanks, Mommy."

References

1 Wilder, Laura Ingalls. **Little House on the Praire**. Rev. ed. New York: HarperCollins, 1953, Print.

2 *The Magic School Bus*. BPS. KAEL, Mesa, AZ. 1995-1997. Television.

3 **101 Dalmations**. Dir. Clyde Geronimi, Hamilton S. Luske, Wolfgang Reitherman. The Walt Disney Company, 1992. VHS.

4 Berenstain, S., & Berenstain, J. *Berenstain Bears*. New York: Random House. 1962-2013

5 Kurcinka, Mary Sheedy. **Raising Your Spirited Child**. New York: HarperPerennial, 1991, Print.

6 *The Holy Bible: Revised Standard Version*. New York: Harper & Brothers, 1952. Print.

7 Leatham, E. Rutter. "Grace." **My Book of Favorite Prayers**. Ed. Majorie Newman. Minneapolis: Augsburg. 1990. Print.

CPSIA information can be obtained
at www.ICGtesting.com
Printed in the USA
FFOW01n1903081115
18427FF

9 781634 135641